Don Roberts' poetry is extraordinary; it is informative, instructional, and entertaining. Some of the themes of his diverse poetry include self-motivation, career choices/opportunities, personal/family relationships, morality, personal/family values, spirtuality, work ethics, community/service involvement, patriotism, citizenship, and education.

It is evident that some of Roberts' poetry reflects his personal experiences, and through his experiences he conveys meaningful messages to all his readers.

I highly endorse the publication of Mr. Roberts' poetry. People who read it or hear it will certainly benefit from its rich and powerful messages. Indeed, Roberts' poetry is "special"—his readers will truly be touched.

Bertha Taylor-Escoffery, Ph.D.
Assistant Professor of English
Norfolk State University
Norfolk, Virginia

. . .It is full of wisdom, warmth, and much food for thought for today's youth (and old folks, too!). Your sensitivity and sincerity come through brilliantly, and I expect it will be well-received upon publication.

Brenda H. Andrews, Publisher
The New Journal & Guide
Norfolk, Virginia

TO LIVE BY

Don Roberts

Hampton Roads Publishing Company, Inc.
134 Burgess Lane
Charlottesville, VA 22902
Or call: (804) 296-2772
    FAX: (804) 296-5096

If you are unable to order this book from your local bookseller, you may order directly from the publisher. Call 1-800-766-8009, toll-free.

Drawings by Sherman Edwards
Cover design by Patrick Smith

ISBN 1-878901-55-9

10 9 8 7 6 5 4 3 2

Printed in the United States of America

Dedication

God, thank you for the inspiration.
Varna, thank you for your patience.
Kristen, Dawn, and Kevin, thank you for the ideas.
V.K.T., Bob, Bertha, Mamie, Cornell, Chester, Ava, Sybil,
Les and Beryl, thank you for your support.
Sherman, thank you for your great drawings
at a moment's notice.

Table of Contents

Part IV
Cashin' In

Part V
Special People

Part VI
The "Deal"

Part VII
Black History Play for a Class or Group

Introduction

Rap. Some adults sound like they're spitting when they say the word. But most kids say it with a smile. Many can name dozens of rap stars and recite intricate rap lyrics, some of which are ten times longer than a traditional song. I admit that I was among those who thought rap would die a painful yet deserved death back in the early '80s. How wrong I was. Kids forced radio and music\TV programmers to make room for it. The fact is that our kids *listen* intensively to rap music. And, consequently, many rap performers are their heroes. Not our doctors, lawyers, scholars and businessmen—the rap stars.

When I noticed my oldest daughter memorizing some intricate and questionable lyrics, I knew something had to be done. Censorship wasn't the answer—programming was. The trick was how to get some other stuff in her ears and in other kids' ears—rap with a message, *Rap to Live By*.

My first serious attempt at "rappin'" was my rip-off of Jazzy Jeff and the Fresh Prince's hit back in '87-'88, "Parents Just Don't Understand." I transcribed it—line for line—three hand-written pages! I then transformed it into my own version—"Kids Don't Understand." Took me two or three weeks to memorize it. I suddenly had new respect for rappers. Whenever I performed it, the kids listened, laughed, and applauded! I knew I was on to something. The trick was coming up with topics, writing them in rap form that's easily adaptable to a jammin' beat, then performing them at the appropriate time. All the topics in this book are either true stories from my experiences as a television news reporter and anchorman or composites of a variety of experiences that I have had or have heard my kids—Kris, Dawn, and Kevin—talking about.

The themes vary, but the common chord is the positive and motivational message.

There's something here for kids of all ages and backgrounds. If I have two favorites, the first is "Special." Whenever I perform it, I urge people to "take the pop quiz on life. . .ask yourself these questions and your answers will prove to you that you are special." The second is "King" (about Martin Luther), which came about as I found myself in a position of having to justify why we honor him every January.

The goal of the book? Top help me buy a new Bronco! Just kidding. Seriously, I just want to prove to myself and to the institutional and professional "doubters" that *all* kids are reachable if we simply try harder to speak their language.

Part I

Serious Stuff

SPECIAL

What is unique about you. . .Are you one of a kind?
Of the billions in this world, only one of you to find?

Check your hand, your finger, look at the print.
It's special to you—every one is different.

Your face, your hair, skin color and size. . .
Even twins are different. . .and it's no surprise.

But are you different for a reason. . .do you have a gift?
Is there something about you that you might have missed?

A talent for music, piano or voice?
Or medicine, mechanics, or all—your choice.

Or maybe it's something on another scale. . .
The ability to teach, to serve or to nail?

If you know what your talent is—then get busy!
If you don't, keep looking 'til your search makes you dizzy.

Your talent makes you different from all the rest. . .
Can't find it? Search on! Put yourself to the test.

It's a gift from God. . .He expects you to use it.
Let your talent blossom or it'll die—you'll lose it.

It's meant to be shared. . .That's part of the deal.
It makes you special. . .Your talent is real.

So later, when you die, God may ask you. . .
"What did you do with the talent I gave you?"

Will you say—"Gee, I didn't know, not much. . ."
Or will you say- "See all the people I've touched?"

REASONS

I'm a firm believer that everything happens for a reason.
The extra special thing happens at a date—time—and season.

Your challenge is to recognize it and figure out what it means.
And learn from the experience—let it help you realize your dreams.

CHOICES

From the time you wake up. . .until you go to bed
You hear these "little voices"—rumbling 'round in your head—

"Do this" or "do that". . .Or—what should you wear?
From the food you want to eat. . .To how to style your hair.

You make hundreds of "choices"—every day of your life.
Some of them are automatic. . .others can cause you strife.

You may "sweat"— when choosing—to "do the 'right' thing."
Or if you choose what's wrong—consequences it'll bring.

Some "choices" are made for you. . .at least until you're grown.
Others are left up to you. . .you've gotta make 'em on your own.

And, as you grow older, you'll have to make more. . .
Of the "choices" for now. . .Through life's final score.

So, it's very important that you learn something now. . .
To help with the "basics" . . .deciding "what". . .and "how". . .

And "who with" and "why". . .You're gonna do what you do.
Because whatever happens, you have to answer to *you*.

Among your many choices. . .Whether to join the "party crowd."
Those guys have good times—much fun—and they can get loud.

It can be hard to study, when your friends are "chillin',"
But when the test comes around, will you also be "illin'"?

Those "zero's" can hurt, and you could have scored an "ace"?
And doin' less than your best—is stupid, let's face (it).

Sorry—life ain't easy. . . It can be tough for teens.
The pressure is high. . .and often more than it seems.

Take the clothes you wear. . .Got to have those "B-K's". . .
At 90 dollars a pop? And you expect mom to pay?

The baggy shorts and the jeans. . .You think you need to be cool?
Stop and think for a minute. . .Who really made this rule?

You can choose for yourself on how "down" you will be. . .
Just know that threads cover up the real person you don't see.

When I was a teen. . .not too long ago. . .
Almost 20 years now—whoa, 20 years? I think so.

Ten dollars was a lot for shoes that fit!
Those "Jack Percells" were nice! You might call them "zits."

But I still had fun. . .made friends, and played sports. . .
Didn't worry 'bout shoes. . .and the jokes I'd ignore.

Pop said don't worry 'bout small things like shoes.
We were buying a house to end the apartment blues.

Pop *chose* to own real estate over having a big car.
It meant pinching pennies but it's the best choice by far.

That meant tough times then. . .for a reward to come later.
He said "the harder you work will make the reward much greater."

At first I thought, "Yeah, dad must be crazy. . ."
Stay home and work, when I could run with the ladies?

I had chores to do. . .A lot of washing and scrubbing;
They called me "momma's boy" 'cause I didn't go clubbin'.

I missed of lot of dances with all the "fine babes". . .
'Cause I had to do homework. . .I felt like a slave.

Pop told me to think. . ."Girls will always be there!"
He said I had to be strong, learn a skill, to prepare. . .
For the future

In the heat of the moment, and you're thinking about sex!
When the moment is right. . .you can't wait for what's next.

You'll make a *choice* that could result in. . .maybe:
The responsibility of caring for a baby.

It goes back to *choices*. . .You gotta know what to choose.
And if you choose to wait on sex, how you can't lose.

And when you want to escape it all and take a flight,
Light up some "herb" or crack—get high tonight. . .

It'll be your *choice*. . .well, at least the *first* time. . .
'Cause if you get hooked, it'll take control of your mind.

If "just saying 'no'" is corny, then just say yes. . .
To life, and health. . .and simply being your best.

You have the power. And you'll want to choose well.
'Cause when you do it right it's easier to excel.

YOUNG (Too young to die)

I can run a mile and not get winded.
Party all night if they extend it.

Dodge the traffic—and not get hit
Sing with "the boys" 'cause my tenor will fit.

I can eat anything and not get fat.
Drink 'til I'm blue and be done with that.

If I get sick—it won't last long.
Never broke a bone 'cause my body is strong.

I don't have a worry—not even about cash.
If I need some, I'll check mom's stash.

Life is great and I'm not trying
So I'm not entertaining any thoughts about
dying.

I'm too young to die. . .I haven't lived yet.
What can happen to me? Nothing, I'll bet.

It seems nothing bad ever happens to me.
If I'm sick early—I'm better by three.

That's why I can't understand Joey.
He caught some illness and he was slowly—

Wasting away in a hospital room—
I kept reminding myself—I've got to visit him soon.

A little while ago we were shooting b-ball.
He blocked my shot and I wanted the "call."

And then he felt weak—and he couldn't breathe.
He was sweating hard and weak in the knees.

Not too long after that, my friend Joey died.
My best buddy—gone! Of course I cried.

I couldn't believe it. He was just like me.
Livin' the life. Havin' fun—no worry.

Joey caught AIDS from messin' round with a girl. . .
He wasn't careful while she "rocked his world."

He didn't think it could ever happen to him.
But it did. . .
and now he's gone.

So suddenly I don't feel so invincible.
I'm not taking chances but it's the principle.

If it happened to him—could it happen to me?
And I thought *we'd* live forever—

QUESTIONS
(It's "cool" to be curious)

Everything starts
With an idea.
Somebody says, "Can I do that?"
It doesn't matter
Whatever it is. . .
Skyscrapers or even knickknacks.

Did you ever
Look at a bridge
And wonder how it holds the weight?
Somebody saw a
Serious need. And
Their effort to fill it was great.

Are you amazed
By personal computers?
And how they store information?
Whoever thought
Of combining the chips
And plastic had a great revelation.

How is it that
You take a pill. . .
To ease some pain in your head?
What causes the spark
That is life? And
Why, when you lose it, you are dead?

It's cool to be
Curious, my friend. . .
'Cause learning stuff can be much fun.
Feel free to ask
Any questions 'cause
When you don't, that's so dumb.

How 'bout the car
That you came in. . .
Who or what put it together?

The clothes you wear—
Just stop and think. . .
How do they make polyester?

How does a telephone
Carry your voice
From one place to another?
And why are we
Born *live* and not
In an egg—from your mother?

Crystal clear glass—
From where does it come?
And the stone they call a diamond?
And why are they
So valuable? Gee—
I wish that I could find one.

Questions, Questions!
They seem so tough.
Are the answers that complicated?
Don't be surprised
To learn it can be
Understood by the uninitiated.

Yes it's okay
To poke your nose
Inside a book—maybe two.
If you have a question,
Don't let it hang.
Find the answer—you need 'booboo.

It's cool to be
Curious, my friend,
'Cause learning stuff can be much fun.
Feel free to ask
Any questions, 'cause
When you don't that is so dumb.

Sure you have to
Go through the process
And take it one step at a time.
You cannot solve
The problems of the world
Overnight, or just in your mind.

Just keep asking
All your questions
And don't stop 'til you find "why". . .
And don't be afraid
To ask "what" and "where"
And "who," "how," and "when"—then try. . .

To make something
On your own, and
Make it something we all need.
Something that
Can help the poor
Live better, like bounty from a seed.

An electric car
That doesn't pollute. . .
Now that is a winning idea.
Or how 'bout a way
To turn trash to cash
Legally?—You've got a career!

What good is your talent
If all you want
Is to make a trip to the bank.
Ease someone's pain,
Help the hungry
Find peace! And we'll have you to thank.

Whatever you do,
Please don't stop
Asking questions and learning what's new.
Forget the dummies
And all the fools
'Cause with knowledge they can't touch you.

It's cool to be
Curious, my friend. . .
'Cause learning stuff can be much fun.
Feel free to ask
Any questions, 'cause
When you don't, that is so dumb.

CAREERS

Be a Doctor, heal the sick.
Use my skill and get rich quick.

Be a Lawyer, take 'em to court.
Sue their pants off—just for sport.

How 'bout hoops? Play Basketball?
Tennis or golf could be my call.

Be a Teacher—help kids learn.
Do it for love, not for what I'll earn.

Every day it's what I hear.
"Got to think about a career!"

Mom says when I go to school no more,
I'll be moving out the door.

A-ten-hut! The Military?
Macho man? It is very—

Tough to hang with all the travel.
Good career—if I can handle (it).

Hear the call to preach the Word?
Want to inspire—Help out, serve?

I don't know what I want to do.
Soon enough I'll get a clue.

Gotta be something to pay the bills
And let me use all my skills.

Don't like school? Skipping class?
Keep that up. I'll pump some gas.

With no hope for the future.
Nickel jobs will only suit 'cha.

Everyday it's what I hear!
"Got to think about a career!"

Mom says when I go to school no more
I'll be moving out that door.

And of course I gotta have the cash!
Enough to live well—don't need it to flash.

I just hope that whatever I do
Will make me happy and productive too.

LOVE YOURSELF

Love yourself! In an unselfish way.
Be your own best friend on this and every day.

Love yourself with the best love you've got.
'Cause through thick and thin you'll need love a lot.

Love yourself when no one else wants to.
Even when the chill of loneliness grips you.

Love yourself when no one else can,
When your attitude is too ugly to stand.

Self-love at its best, starts into motion
A chain of events like a wave from the ocean.

Self-love cleans out all selfish feeling
For that is contrary to love's true meaning.

Self-love leaves no room for false pride.
It's quiet confidence that knocks doubts aside.

Self-love is honesty with yourself and others.
It's giving freely to your sisters and brothers.

You'll have a glow that radiates like the sun.
People will want to be around you for fun.

You'll find that your love will put you at ease.
It's an inner confidence that makes work a breeze.

When you love yourself, you'll do your best.
You won't be satisfied with mediocrity or less.

Everything and everyone that you may touch
Will reflect your kindness—it'll mean that much.

You're kind of shy and don't know how to get going?
"Loving yourself" sounds weird and annoying?

Just look in the mirror and like what you see.
And then tell yourself: *"I love me!*

CONTROL (be in)

I feel the power. I'm climbing the tower.
The choice is mine!

The view from up here is very clear.
I'll do just fine.

I'm in control!

I am the pilot of my life ship.
I set the course. . .

I'm going places, will see many faces
on positive force. . .

I'm in control!

I want to do things and see what life brings.
Expand my mind.

The weight is on me. I am the boss, you see.
I handle the grind.

I'm in control!

No one can make me or try to take me
Where I don't want to go.

I do my own thing—my song I sing.
All the words I know.

I'm in control!

If I mess up. . .Yes I will 'fess up
to my mistakes. . .

But, I won't "lean," or beg for your green.
I'll make my breaks.

I'm in control!

Don't need your drug—I'm not a slug.
So to you—goodbye!

The future is mine; I've got the time.
And I plan to fly.

I'm in control!

The sky's my limit. I'll fly through it
At the speed of light.

And I can't wait, I don't plan to skate.
'Cause my future is bright!

I'm in control!

LOVE MYSELF (rap-a-long)
(—*Elementary*—)

I LOVE. . .I love
      MYSELF. . .myself
I LOVE. . .I love
      MYSELF!. . .myself

I LOOK GOOD. . .I look good
      AND I KNOW IT. . ..and I know it.
THAT'S WHY I. . .that's why I
      AM PROUD TO SHOW IT. . .am proud to show it.

DRUGS ARE DUMB. . .drugs are dumb
      THEY'RE NOT FOR PLAY. . ..not for play.
I'LL DO FINE. . .I'll do fine
      THE NATURAL WAY. . .the natural way

I WANT TO BE COOL. . .I want to be cool
      SOME OF THE TIME. . .some of the time
BUT LET ME TAKE. . .but let me take
      CARE OF MY MIND. . .care of my mind

I CAN BE HIP. . .I can be hip
      AND HAVE SOME FUN. . .and have some fun
BUT I WANT TO "GROW". . .want to grow
      BE NUMBER 1!. . .be number 1!

I'M LIKE A ROSE. . .I'm like a rose
      STILL IN THE BUD. . .still in the bud
I'M GOING TO BLOSSOM!. . .going to blossom
      I'M NOT A DUD!. . .I'm not a dud.

I AM BEAUTIFUL. . .I am beautiful
      AND I AM PROUD. . .and I am proud
I'M GONNA MAKE IT!. . .gonna make it
      I'LL SAY IT LOUD!. . .say it loud
I LOVE. . .I love
      MYSELF!. . .myself
I LOVE. . .I love
      MYSELF!. . .myself

I LOVE MYSELF!. . .I love myself
I LOVE MYSELF!. . .I love myself

OH YEAH!!!!!!!!!!

****

LOVE MYSELF (rap-a-long)
(—Middle and High School—)

I LOVE. . .I love
    MYSELF. . .myself
I LOVE. . .I love
    MYSELF!. . .myself

I LOOK GOOD. . .I look good
    AND I KNOW IT. . ..and I know it.
THAT'S WHY I. . .that's why I
    AM PROUD TO SHOW IT. . .am proud to show it.

GET TO KNOW ME. . .Get to know me
    BE MY BUDDY. . .Be my buddy
I'M PRETTY COOL. . .I'm pretty cool
    NO FUDDY DUDDY. . .No fuddy duddy

I CAN BE SERIOUS. . .I can be serious
    'CAUSE I WANT TO BE READY. . .'cause I want to be rea
FOR WHEN THE DOOR OPENS. . .for when the door opens
    AND I CAN ROCK STEADY. . .and I can rock steady

DRUGS ARE DUMB. . .Drugs are dumb
    THEY'RE NOT FOR PLAY. . .They're not for play
I'LL DO FINE. . .I'll do fine
    THE NATURAL WAY. . .the natural way

I AM SPECIAL. . .I am special
    HAVE A LOT TO GIVE. . .Have a lot to give
GOTTA LOT TO DO. . .Gotta lot to do
    I WANT TO LIVE!. . .I want to live!

I'LL DO A GOOD JOB. . .I'll do a good job
    NO MATTER THE TASK. . .No matter the task

I'LL DO IT RIGHT. . .I'll do it right
     YOU DON'T HAVE TO ASK. . .You don't have to ask

JUST WATCH ME WORK. . .Just watch me work
     PUT YOUR TRUST IN ME. . .Put your trust in me
I'M NOT A JERK. . .I'm not a jerk
     I'M GREAT—YOU'LL SEE. . .I'm great—you'll see

I LOVE. . .I love
     MYSELF!. . .myself
I LOVE. . .I love
     MYSELF!. . .myself

I LOVE MYSELF!. . .I love myself
I LOVE MYSELF!. . .I love myself

     OH YEAH!!!!!!!!!!!

Part II
Knuckleheads

MIKEY
Stay in School

I know a little guy named Mikey. . .he sports the high-top
"Nikey."
He also likes the movies especially those that are made by
Spike Lee.

He thinks he is so cool. He likes to hook from school.
He says it is so boring so he breaks the golden rule.

Now Mikey is no dummy. He and books were very chummy.
He could work his math so well in fact it wasn't even funny.

He could read his books so fast, that his homework would not last.
All he had to do was try and surely he would have passed.

But Mikey was so "fly," that he didn't even try.
Thought books were for squares so he told the school "bye-bye."

Mikey did drop out 'cause he wanted to hang out
He works now at McDonald's and he's finding what life's about.

At 4-25 an hour, he can't afford to shower.
He stays home with his mother and he feels he has no power.

So another job he takes. He sweeps the floor at "Jakes."
This job pays 5 bucks, so it's not much more he makes.

If he wants a real promotion, he's got to get the notion,
That he needs a high school diploma and a skill—that's no joke, son.

'Cause in this day and time, computers tow the line.
You've got to know your stuff, or you'll get left behind.

And if you have the smarts, don't break your mother's heart.
Stay in school and do the work so you can be a part of. . .

The happy people who do what they want to
'Cause when you have the knowledge, it's so much easier to—

Make a little money so you and your "honey"
Can have a nice car and home and play a lot of gin rummy.

And if you have the talent, then you had better use it!
'Cause if you let it waste away, then you will surely lose it!

If you're smart—okay! No need to shy away.
Friends call you a "nerd" then tell them to eat some hay!

Just don't be like that Mikey. . .you can still have your Nikey.
Work for all the things you want, and you'll enjoy them
more—that's likely!

Feel good about success! Be proud to do your best!
Dare to be somebody great and you'll always pass the test!

KIESHA

Let me tell you 'bout a girl named Kiesha.
And if you get the chance, she'd like to meet 'cha.
  She likes the fancy tennis shoes,
  Clothes, and wild hairdos. . .
But Kiesha also has a brain she likes to tweek-a.

Kiesha has a reputation for being nosey.
She sticks her pug in your business like a rosey
  She's very curious. . .
  She'll make you furious. . .
She just likes knowledge and that's no jokey.

Now, Kiesha never ever missed a day of school.
'Cause being absent to her is so uncool.
  She has to see her girls. . .
  Find out who rocked whose world. . .
And if she's not sick, why "act the fool"?

Watch her eyes light up when she reads a book.
Kiesha's brain starts spinnin' and she'll look
  Like a wild woman danglin'. . .
  Her jewels would be janglin'. . .
'Cause she's excited by the stories in the book.

Kiesha has some girlfriends who are kind of cute.
And all the guys try to squeeze their "juicy fruit."
  The girls like the attention. . .
  And some do things I can't mention. . .
And when Kiesha said "no," she got the boot.

It hurt Kiesha's feelings to be alone
Her girlfriends would not call her on the telephone.
  They said she couldn't hang. . .
  Couldn't run with the gang. . .
And so it was her choice to be unknown.

Now, here's another side to her story.
Although Kiesha didn't study for the glory.
  Whenever she took a test. . .

The "A" showed her best. . .
And she made the honor roll with Duke and Corey.

Kiesha kept this up through the 12th grade.
And by then, she was ready to get "paid."
   Not talking "chump" change. . .
   'Cause she's broadened her range. . .
Kiesha wants "college" and with her grades, she's got it made.

So, for homegirl, school may have been hard
'Cause she worked, didn't chase boys in the yard.
   She dreamed of being a doc. . .
   Didn't want to punch a clock. . .
And she earned that scholarship to Harvard.

YOUNG MOTHER

When you learned you were pregnant were you filled with joy?
Happy to give life to a lil' girl or boy?

Thankful for the blessings a baby can bring. . .
So excited about the child, that you wanted to sing?

Or were you depressed when you heard the news?
Angry about this burden that you did not choose?

Cursing the father for his mistake. . .
And mad at yourself for precautions you did not take?

Or was this on purpose—you wanted the baby?
To show you've grown up to be quite the young lady?

This brand new child—will be all your own?
This baby is yours—he's proof that you are grown?

Whatever the reason, the child is now a fact!
That you have to deal with—there's no looking back.

So what does this mean—how will your life change?
Classes, and parties—will friends treat you strange-ly.

It's up to you to keep your life on track. . .
Take one step forward, not two steps back.

It's twice as hard now to provide for two.
But you can do it—if you really want to.

Just think of your child and all that he needs.
He depends on you to plant the good seeds.

And to help them grow so he'll be strong and healthy
and smart and talented, productive and even wealthy!

If you succeed, he'll be in your debt.
He'll love you to death—and he will never forget. . .

That "mother cared for me—she gave me the best!"
And in doing so—you, Mom, will possess. . .

More love for yourself. So let it be recorded:
That for sacrifices made, you will be richly rewarded!

CRACK MOMMA

(on trial)

Damn she was good. . .she sure could move fast. . .
Ducked all the news cameras and ran right past (us. . .)

She zipped through the hearing and showed some remorse
The judge paid it no mind and proceeded on course

He set the date for when she'll be back
For a hearing to explain her apparent lack. . .

Of love for the little girl she gave birth to.
She was born brain dead. . .crack in her blood too.

The charge, a felony: neglect and abuse. . .
The penalty—prison. . .the judge will choose.

If the child dies—the prognosis is grim
Mom could get more time to pay for this sin

Mom didn't want her face on the news. . .
Slipped out a side door. . .planned that well too.

We just wanted to ask—"Didn't you know
The risk to you and your baby from Blow?"

How dare we reporters have cameras in place. . .
What was her crime? Leaving a baby to face. . .

A life with brain damage. . .or no life at all. . .
Because it's too weak and cannot not withdraw. . .

From crack. Mom was going home, having made bail,
But she cursed newspeople for telling her tale.

Mom's back in court on August 23rd.
From the media the last she's not heard.

She'll no doubt duck the cameras again.
Our showing her face is some kind of sin.

At one thing she's good. . .she sure can move fast.
She'll duck the news cameras and run right past us. . .

WOMAN WASTED

I know a smart woman. . .She's almost kin to me.
She could be a doctor, a lawyer, or Ph.d.

Yes she is that smart—her mind is quick.
But she used to get caught in that welfare trick.

Now some really need the social services' aid. . .
But others—like this woman—treat it like "kool aid."

You know what she's doing? Now this is no joke!
She's messin' with drugs—her favorite is coke.

She has six children! A family that needs her!
But all that's on her mind is gettin' crack to please her!

She thought she could handle it. . .Could quit, say no!
But when the rent was due the man said she had to go.

She spent all the money on liquor and Blow.
Forgot about the family, cared nothing about them, so. . .

They took her kids away 'cause she made a choice. . .
Heard the call of the drug—not her child's voice.

So, we read the newspapers, the obituary section
'Cause today or tomorrow—her name they will mention.

"Dead of an 'O.D.'". . .Killed at a wild party.
And her kids will grow up—knowing her name? Not hardly.

PROJECTS
(livin' in the. . .)

Whenever my teacher talks about me, she says:
"Oooh, he's such a nice kid!"
She says I'm so smart and I do my work
Like I was a little "whiz."

She always talks about how goody I am
And how I'm easy to get along with.
But it ticks me off when she goes on and says:
"But he lives in the projects."

Like, what does that mean? To me it's just a place
Where people who don't have the cash. . .
Have to live—and until they get on their feet,
They've got to put up with some trash.

But it's where I live; it's not what I am!
So I wish she'd stop treating me funny.
And stop being surprised when I show up to school
With my lunch and a little bit of money.

So what! I'm from the projects—it's just a zip code-
It's not *what I am!*
The only reason drug dealers hang out there
Is because some politicians don't give a damn.

Yeah some of my neighbors are "welfare queens"
But they're exceptions and not the rule.
There're nice old folks, young families trying to make it,
And my buddies who are pretty cool.

Yeah I live in Roberts' Garden, Jeffrey Wilson, Newsome Park,
But that doesn't mean I'm handicapped.
I know I can learn like any other kid
Give me a chance! My mind ain't trapped!

As soon as I mention where it is I live
I hear her mumblin' "Oh—that's too bad."
Bust it, Babe—I don't need your pity or your pattin'!
Just because there're some things I've never had.

Yeah, some of my friends don't have a mom or pop
Who care about them like mine do.
And they speak their own language which ain't the King's English
But it gets us where we're goin', too.

You say I'm poor, underprivileged, and deprived?
Well, that's funny, and it's news to me.
I know we don't have a whole lot of cash
But we have what we need so I'm happy.

The projects? It's where I live; it's not what I am!
So I wish you'd stop treating me funny.
And stop being surprised when I show up to school
with my lunch and a little bit of money.

I'm not a drug dealer. I'm just a kid,
And because of where I live, I need a break?
Well, that's cool. But I'm ready to eat up the knowledge!
All I ask is that you give me a fair shake.

THEY SAY

What makes you one of the few "select men"?
You don't want to know because "they" say, in ten—

Years, by 2000, "they" say—you'll be dead!
Shot by a "brother," a robber, dopehead.

Or "they" say you'll spend some time in a jail.
They'll put you away since, at life, you have failed.

"They" say you'll be doped up from getting sky "high."
Your life won't matter since success passed you by.

You may "wave the hanky" and choose the gay life
Or get AIDS the other way—playin' around on your wife.

"They" say your future is not all that bright.
And "they" have been known to be proven right.

So what do you think about what "they" are saying?
Do you really care or are you busy playing—

The role that "they" have laid out for you. . .
Love to party—"get over"—and be cool.

You even dabble in drugs to get cash.
Don't smoke it or stick it! Too smart for that trash!

But you wheel and deal—selling poison to a brother.
Acting like a businessman! The dollar is your "lover."

"Seven out of ten"—that is pretty bad. . .
And will "they" be right? Or will you get mad?

Get mad at yourself and refuse to play the game
Of failing to achieve—yourself you'll have to blame.

So is it possible to prove "they" are wrong?
Will you buckle down and show you are strong?

Choose life over death, and make your life count.
Prove that "they" are wrong—that you know what life's about!

THE G-N-B's
("Go-nowhere-brothers")

Go-no-where, been-no-where, going-no-where-brothers. . .
All they do is hurt one another.
Cause nothing but heartache for their mothers.
The Go-no-where, been-no-where, going-no-where-brothers.

For the sake of brevity call them "G-N-B's."
It's not the kind of club in which you want to be.
They "go-no-where"—not 'cause they don't have money.
Their outlook on life is negative—that's not funny.

They live for today like there's no tomorrow.
Sleep in class and on a test they borrow.
When you try to help them, they want to quarrel.
Means nothing to them to cause you some sorrow.

When they're on the street, they shoot to kill!
Hurting your body—for them—is a cheap thrill.
Why is it that they lack good will?
Their only view of life seems to come from a pill.

The G-N-B's have no respect for a lady.
They use her only for sex and makin' babies.
Don't hang around to be a daddy—are you crazy?
Can't hold down a job because they're lazy.

Do you know a guy who fits this discrip?
Someone who causes problems with his "lip"?
A professional "hard head" who can't get a grip?
Someone who is lost—who can't seem to fit?

Leave him alone if he doesn't want to try.
Don't push him hard or you'll get a black eye.
But then—we can't just give up on the guy.
We can meet him half way but we *have to try*!

JAIL

Remember when you knocked that kid upside the head?
You rolled when you scared "grandma" out of her bed.
Snatched that pocket book to get some quick cash.
Grabbed that lady's jewels and made a mad dash.

Boys-in-the-hood think that you are too cool. . .
Won't get caught cause "Jake ain't no fool."
Dodge the bullet now, but will you always prevail?
Homeboy, in a matter of time you're going to jail.

Four walls in a cell—that's only 8 by 8. . .
Share that with three other guys who can't wait. . .
For fresh meat. You'll take the place of their lady.
Bend over, slim, 'cause they're bigger than you baby.

Just think—ten years of being Duke's punk.
Oh, you're too tough? Think you can hide like a monk?
Prison won't be bad 'cause you know how to "rock"!
You'll be a big man in the "big house" as you watch the clock.

What about your friends out here living the life?
They'll forget about you and don't expect your wife . . .
And kids to wait for you—Be there with open arms?
To welcome you home after you've been away so long?

And all because you had to be cool as ice. . .
Downed a little 'erb, crack and wine—it was nice.
Banged the heads of anybody that got in your way?
Shot the old man, then—told him "have a nice day."

And when you go to jail—they won't give a damn.
Rehab? What's that? Learn a trade? Forget that—man.
In jail you'll be so busy trying to stay alive.
Fightin' killers who've got your sentence "times five."

It's so funny now 'cause you are livin' the life.
And when they mess with your game, you cut 'em with your knife.
C'mon brother—man—is that all you know?
To bang heads, grab bags, and get high on Blow?

There is a better way if you'll just give me the time.
Can't talk now? Then, let me drop a dime.
Duke, hear me now—cause I don't want you to fail.
You can listen to me here or call me from jail.

Here are 10 reasons why
You should be a drug dealer!
Crimeline will pay me big bucks when I squeal-a on you!

Number 2:
You'll be a target that's moving. . .
For police or other dealers bent on improving their aim.

It's a game. . .
For car dealers who want your cash. . .
They'll send their kids to school while they treat you like trash. . .

And in a flash
The undertakers will get rich off you guys.
When they bury your brothers who were shot in drive-by's.

Your body size?
Casket makers have got you down pat;
While you're in it, we'll see your Nikeys and Malcolm-X hat.

You got that?
Well, get this: you'll learn chemistry
And you may blow yourself up in your own pharmacy.

Yo! G!
Those Columbians who grow coke—don't get dirty.
They thank you for doin' it, dummy, but you'll be dead by age 30.

But don't worry!
'Cause we always need bodies for donations.
Your heart, liver and kidneys will help the people 'cross the nation.

The population—
In prison—like old dealers Jake and Earl?
They'll make space for you cause you'll be their girl.

And in my world—
When I write about the good news that's "class". . .
I'll love reporting how the neighbors kicked your —-.

FRINGIES

(Fringe benefits—reasons and rewards for not using drugs)

You can make 500 buck a week by just standing
on the corna'. . .
Or you can work for Mick-ey D's 'round the way, flippin'
burgers or pouring soda.

All you have to do is "peep the man" in his bubble
or unmarked car.
And sing like a bird to let Slim know: 5-0"
is not too far.

Or you can hustle for about 2 weeks to make what "G" can
get on a good day.
But this chump change will be worth more to you
than blood money from Be' Be'.

Yeah, the drug dollar is long, and you can't go wrong when you've
got plenty of cash. . .
But what good is it all if you can't stand tall while society
treats you like trash?

You need the "fringies," babe, the benefits you get from doin'
somethin' good on your own. . .
The fringies—babe—can't put a price on them, you'll understand when you're grown.

Yeah, you got a good thing, and in just two weeks, you'll
pay cash for your Beamer.
17-year-old kid with a 50-k car—tinted glass, phone, bar.
It's a dreamer.

So why should you give up that good thing and fight the
grease for your money?
Well, for one: it's safer to work legit, than to duck bullets
from your buddy!

And why should you cut off your cash flow—and slave at
Quik Chik for your pay?
'Cause if you work it right, you'll get enough cash, and your
momma will see you another day.

Let the Man "use" you—at his minimum wage—but let this
be the start!
Go ahead and pay your dues—for now—and later you will
get the best part—
of. . .

The "fringies," babe—the benefits you get from doin'
something on your own.
The fringies, babe—can't put a price on them—you'll understand it when you're grown.

The "fringies," babe—it's a feeling you get from your toes
to your brain.
The fringies, babe, benefits like knowledge 'cause that's the
power to win the game!

TV NEWS

I am here to plead with you to *stay the hell off TV news!*
'Cause every time I turn around I see Fila tennis shoes.

They're on some brother's feet as he's lying flat out upon a
stretcher.
With a hole in his head because he forgot to duck, I'm willing
to betcha.

Naw, that's not it, that's not the real reason I'm upset
with you.
It's just that every time I look I see a brother
dead too!

Behind some stupid stuff like girlfriends, clothes and especially
Blow,
Another young life wasted—his mother cries out *"Why is this
so?"*

In school, you brought a gun to show everyone that you are
macho. . .
They busted your butt—put you on TV to say that you were
not so—

Smart as you thought you were—let's face it that was really
dumb.
Scaring people ain't the best or safest way to go out and have
some fun.

But why do you have to be on TV doing something
Bad!?
Sometimes it's the only way to get on the air that makes me
mad!

But try my way—do something to help out in the neighborhood.
And even if you didn't get on TV it'll make you feel real
good!

You made life better for another person—yes, you did your best!
And you helped yourself to become a better person—that is the test.

And think of those who love you—mom and pop, sister and brother. . .
Think of how they'd cry if you were dead, in jail or running for cover.

Otherwise I'm pleading with you to *stay the hell off TV news*. . .
'Cause the rest of us don't need to see your raggedy tennis shoes.

Please don't be that brother carried away lyin'
on a stretcher.
With a hole in his head because he forgot to duck, I'm willing to betcha.

If you can't get on TV for doing something good—then don't get on at all!
I'd rather look at *nothing* than to see you in chains
up against the wall.

Think more of yourself—than the negative stereotype they think you are.
Prove 'em wrong by doin' the right thing—and maybe you'll be a TV star.

MAKE THE NEWS

Here's a tip on how you can make the news.
No, I'm not talking about telling me your blues.
I'm talking about 'bout helping you to choose
The happenings in your life that make "good" news.

How often do you hear about a crime nearby.
You reel in shock and ask yourself "why?"
And what's worse is when it happens nearby
To a person in your block who've you've seen and said "hi."

But you didn't know the name of your next-door neighbor . . .
Had never stopped by or bothered to ask a favor.
Have no good times that you can savor—
Said you get around to it maybe sometime later.

Now you ask yourself, how could that happen here?
This nice neighborhood where you've lived for a year?
Kids play freely 'cause you have no fear
But there's something missing—something's just not clear.

Why do criminals pick one block and not another?
Break through your door or threaten your mother?
Take your belongings—and later you discover
No one saw a thing—sorry—can't help, brother.

Get to know that old lady who lives next door
She sees everything as she paces the floor.
How 'bout the new couple that lives at "0-4"
They're new on the block, and friends? They need more.

Friends keep friends from getting into trouble.
"You watch out for mine" and I'll check on your bubble.
And before you know it, crime could decrease by double
Because you care enough to scare off the dude with the stubble.

If you see a child that's headed the wrong way,
It may not be easy to go up to him and say:
"That's 'wrong,' this is 'right,' here's 'why'—okay?"
It might just work—don't let him get away.

In a more organized effort, you could volunteer. . .
"Big Brother & Sisters"—boys clubs—they're here.
If we reach the kids now, maybe in a later year
We'll watch them with pride and have less to fear.

So that is how you can work on good news.
Tell us there's more here than just the blues.
Show us that you want a variety from which to choose
And keep doing the stuff that makes good news.

NEVER
(Going to give up on "hardheads")

Yeah, you think I'm corny—Call me *"Daddy Bug-a-Boo."*
'Cause I'm raggin' on your nerves—sounds like I'm preaching too.

But maybe there's a chance that you might just hear
Some word to change your mind before the bullet hits your ear.

No matter what you say, I won't give up give up on you, gee.
'Cause, when I see you now—it's like I see a little me.

But, if I can make it—I know you can, too!
But, you've got to want it and then go get it, boo boo.

At one time, they say I had a hard head like yours
But I managed to get on track—and I stayed until I scored.

And now it's your turn to get your piece of the pie.
You can do it the right way or you can mess up and die.

Sometimes that's the price that you will have to pay.
But, so much is out here for you—I don't care what they say.

But you gotta *go get it*—Gotta *make your own breaks!*
You don't need handouts 'cause you've got what it takes.

You've just got to believe and then go and take a chance.
And prepare yourself well—for Life, "The Big Dance."

But the kind of chances you take just drive me up the wall.
You get me so frustrated and you make no sense at all.

But, no matter what you do, I won't give up on you, gee.
'Cause when I see you, it's like, I see a little me.

But, if I can make it—I know you can, too.
But, you've got to want it, and then go get it, boo boo.

There are people out here who don't care if you're dead.
And they'll lock up your butt or put a bullet in your head.

They can make it so easy for you to get mugged. . .
Mugged by the Drug sold to you by the thug.

But the final choice is yours and I do care what you do.
'Cause when I get old I'll be depending on you.

You'll be "The Man" in charge and have all the power.
Or you will be dead or locked up in a tower.

I'm scared to death to think that you might not be around. . .
And all the future generations of kids will be light brown.

Cause there won't be any "brothers" to continue our race. . .
You'll all be dead—in jail—doped-out, or flying in space.

No matter what you do, I won't give up on you, gee.
'Cause when I see you, it's like, I see a little me.

But, if I can make it—I know you can, too.
But, you've got to want it, and then go get it, boo boo.

WALK
(With a purpose)

Check out Billybob—why is he walkin' so fast?
He actin' like the competition is trying to pass (him. . .)

I don't hear a fire truck so nothing's burning down.
And the store ain't givin' away nothing free in this town.

But why is Slim Jim steppin' out so quick with a beat?
It's 'cause he's got somewhere to go and people to meet.

He's walking with a purpose—don't have any time to waste.
And he's going to get there and get the goodies to taste.

When you walk with a purpose you won't fall on your face.
Just act like you are on your way to a special place.

If they stop you wanting to know where it is you're going
Just tell em you've got business that you need to be doing.

You've got to walk quickly so you can step over the blocks.
They're the "been-no-where" people who just watch the clock.

Those people dragging their feet and cracking gum—that's annoying!
They've got nowhere to go and so you know they are boring.

Don't have time for doin' nothin'—sittin' 'round talking trash.
Got places-to-go, people-to-see, trying to earn some cash.

When you walk with a purpose you will always be on time.
And when you walk fast you can stimulate your mind. . .

So you'll know what to do when you get where you're going
And take care of the business that you need to be doing.

DRUGS
(Sayin' no to. . .)

Should I get with this program? Or maybe check out
that?
The Just-Say-No-to-Drugs show-down: Is it real or out of
whack?

They say the stuff is bad—that it can scramble
up my brain.
But everybody's doin' it and to me they
act the same.

I really don't need the stuff 'cause I can get high
on my own.
But everybody's doin' it—some kids do it
in their home.

They say the Blow is bad! It'll make you feel
like Superman!
But I wonder what happens when you have to come back
down again?

I could leave the Blow alone and become a street corner
business man!
I can make some serious cash and buy my Beamer or
Trans Am.

I don't know what to do. But I know I gotta make a
choice-choice
I think I need some help or should I listen to the
little voice?

Should I get with this program? Or maybe check out
that one?
I gotta do somethin' 'cause just hangin' ain't that
much fun.

Workin' in an office for The Man sounds
like a drag.
I know!? I'll open a business selling "weaving"
hair by-the-bag.

But I like to use my hands and build things—carpentry,
engineering?
But will all that Math go kick my butt and maybe leave me
screaming?

Whatever it is I do—I want to do it 'cause
I want to.
And not because they tell me. That can't make me 'cause
I'm strong—so. . .

Should I get with this program—or maybe check out
another one?
When it comes to Blow—yo', I don't know!
So I'll let it go—for some other fun.

NO

"Iron Mike" Tyson thought he was in heaven
As he surveyed all the cuties
Just couldn't resist the temptation to
Squeeze on some of their Booties.

He liked their smiles and shapely curves,
And to touch them was no big deal. . .
And besides, they liked all the attention
'Cause Iron Mike was for real.

The girls were blushing, as Mike was flirting,
First with one, then the other.
He would put his arm around this babe,
Then went down the line to another.

Iron Mike was getting all worked up,
And his hormones started jumpin'
He was sweatin' hard and drippin' like
In a weight room when he's pumpin.'

Iron Mike, the champ and millionaire
Was very used to getting his way.
And he needed to take control of somebody
Like he does in the ring for pay.

Meanwhile, Homegirl? She was just so thrilled
That the Champ looked at her twice.
Of all the girls in the pageant, he picked her
And he acted so nice!

Maybe those things they said about Mike
Beating women? A bunch of lies?
He's a superstar with a whole lot of money
And he's cute—just look at those eyes.

So Homegirl forgot what Mama said
And she left common sense at home.
She went for a ride in the champ's limousine
And couldn't believe they were alone!

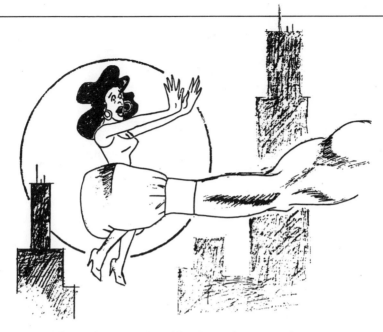

She thought Mike was "cool" when she agreed,
To go where he was stayin'.
He made his move—She said No!
But Iron Mike was not up for playin'.

So Mike Tyson took her! Mike Tyson raped her!
Violated her in the worst way.
If you're a guy, you can't understand that—
No matter what you might say.

It's hard to explain how it feels to be raped—
To be used like a piece of meat.
Your body is your temple, the home of your soul.
And he stomped on hers with his feet.

You say she was a "tease"—who led him on.
So she had to go "do the do?"
Yo-Gee! At what point does a woman's body
Belong completely to you?

A woman should be able to go where she wants—
No one asks for that kind of assault.
Rape is a crime of violence, not sex.
So don't make it sound like her fault.

And don't forget evidence—used by judge and jury
To convict him in the case. . .
But still some guys don't believe he was wrong.
Check that smirk on your face?

Now Iron Mike stands convicted of rape
And in prison he will serve his time. . .
When she says No, Bud, you've got to say Whoa!
Just keep Iron Mike in your mind.

Part III
Funnin'

SHARING

I got a brand new toy today!
And I can't wait to go out to play.

I'll show all the kids that I've got the best.
But then "Mean Gene" will want to put it to the test.

He's too big—he always breaks my stuff.
I don't think he means it, but he sure is rough!

This toy is really special and I want to have fun.
I better play with it now and when he comes—I'll run!

"Mean Gene" is too big to chase after me.
And if he comes runnin' I'll climb up a tree.

If he comes near my house I'll act like I'm dead.
He might believe it 'cause he's a knucklehead.

I never see him playing with any other kids.
I wonder why? Is it something he did?

Mom says "Mean Gene" just wants someone to play with.
He's an "only child" and he has no one to stay with.

I don't know. . .that mean look is in his eye.
I don't know. . .should I give him a try?

Hey, "Mean Gene"—do you want to play?
I'll share my toy with you if you'll be nice today.

GOLDIE
(Rip-off of "Goldilocks"—the untold story)

Have you heard the story about little Goldie Locks?
She ripped off the Bears and almost got her head knocked.

I know you remember when she broke into their home.
She ate up their porridge and then she started to roam. . .

All over the house until she found some chairs.
Didn't like mom's and pop's, but sat in Baby Bear's.

And then this homeless girl suddenly felt like sleeping.
She crawled all over their beds, found one, and started dreaming.

And then the bears came home thinking their porridge was cool.
They noticed something wrong—Poppa Bear was not a fool.

Goldie wasn't shy and she was very, very hungry.
She ate the baby's food and they didn't think it was funny.

Goldie was bold! She even left their chairs rocking.
Except for Baby's—which she broke—and that was shocking.

Now the bears were angry and they wanted to know
Who ate their food, broke a chair—he's got to go!

And then they heard some snoring and none of them was sleeping.
They crept into the bedroom and started a-peeping.

Someone had jumped in Poppa Bear's bed and made a mess,
And someone slept in Momma Bear's bed—who will confess?

But wait! Look at Baby Bear's bed—there is a lump!
And that lump is wiggling. Could this be the chump?

Momma grabbed the phone—she was dialing 9-1-1.
Poppa knew karate—didn't want to use a gun.

Baby Bear screamed when he saw a *little girl!*
Her name was Goldilocks, but he planned to straighten her curl.

Goldie woke up and hollered like the boy in *Home Alone!*
She got up and ran, before the cops surrounded the home.

She didn't even say "thank you" and that wasn't very polite.
I guess she thought the bears would eat her for dinner that night!

LIL' RED
(Riding in the Hood)

Her name was really "Sha-nay-nay"
But friends liked to call her "Little Red"
'Cause she liked to ride on her bike
With a red hood pulled over her head.

It's not that she was bald or anything—
Little Red just liked to be cool.
With the hood on she could hide her face
From ugly boys when she went to school.

Well, on this day this little girl
Had to take a walk before dark.
Her mom asked her to take some food
To her Granny who lived 'cross the park.

Little Red did not think much about
The dangers of walking alone.
She walked fast, and if she needed help
She'd call on her pocket cell-phone.

Little Red knew not to talk to strangers,
But this big hairy guy seemed so nice.
He asked her where she was going,
And she told him without thinking twice.

Willy Wolfe was his name and he was hungry
And he had his mind set on a meal.
He knew where Little Red's Granny lived
And if he got there fast he could steal!

Willy Wolfe ran to Granny's house real fast.
And he knocked her upside her head!
Granny did get in a few licks,
But Wolfy grabbed her out of her bed.

He stuffed Granny in her closet
Then he got dressed up in her clothes.
Wolfy planned to wait for Little Red—
What was he going to do—who knows?

Little Red came in with her basket,
And she quickly saw something was wrong.
She thought Granny looked kind of strange—
Didn't remember her nose being that long.

"You remember my great sense of smell?" Wolfy said.
"That's why your Granny's nose is so big."
"But Granny, I don't remember that fat tummy," said Red.
"It's like you've been eating like a pig."

"And Granny, why are your teeth so yellow?
And your breath is stinking up the place.
Maybe you need to use the bathroom,
And brush your teeth with Crest toothpaste."

Willy Wolfe said, "I don't need this crap."
And he jumped up and tried to grab Little Red.
Red screamed, "Help!" and pulled out her phone,
Tried to call the cops before she was dead.

Crime Dog was tracking Willie Wolfe,
And he was not very far away.
Wolfy had a "rep" as a knucklehead,
And when Crime Dog got the call, he said, "Hey!"

Crime Dog burst into the house real fast,
And he punched Willie Wolfe in the jaw!
Then he got the woman out of the closet.
Little Red cried happy tears, saying "Hey Grandma!"

As the police took Willie Wolfe to jail,
Crime Dog whispered in Little Red's ear.
He said, "You were lucky this time,
But don't ever talk to strangers—you hear?"

KIDS DON'T UNDERSTAND!
(The answer to Jazzy Jeff's hit "Parents Don't Understand")

Now, now calm down, baby, I think our son is okay.
They've got him locked up in jail along with some runaway.

He's trying to grow up too fast. Hard Head thinks he's a
man. . .
They're all the same—they don't listen. . .Kids just don't
understand.

I remember one year when we went school shopping.
They had a sale at K-Mart, and there was no stopping—

Us from grabbing a bargain, double knits looked good, you
know the reversible kind.
And I knew I would find. . .

Some classic shirts with the butterfly collar.
Man—did they look boss, and for only 20 dollars!

But did "knucklehead" appreciate the money we spent?
Nah! he turned up his nose, and that's when I went—

Boy—those tennis shoes are like the ones that I used to wear.
He said "Dad, those are 'zits'—I'll get laughed out of there!."

Mom said, "Sticks and stones will break your bones but
names will never hurt you."
He said, "Mom, you don't know the fellas like I do!"

He kept on crying like a new born baby.
I was tired of this mess and thought that—maybe. . .

When school began he would see we were right.
"Son, it's not how you look, it's who you are inside.

You see, the problem with the boy is he likes to dress like "G-Q,"
But when you make "McDonald's money," that's something
you can't do.

He said that plaid jacket would not fit.
I said, "Hold that 'joint'—go 'head and pack it."

The boy has no taste; I've got to teach him some style
And those "bell-bottom" pants will hit any day now!

It was time for school and my boy looked good.
He'd be the talk of the class, like I knew he would.

And when he got there, all the kids were smiling!
I was proud of my boy, and he was profiling.

But he still complained, saying he needed new styles.
I said, "Boy you've got all you're going to get for while."

He said the kids were laughing as he walked down the hall.
I said, "Boy. . .those kids weren't looking at you at all.

You got to stop thinking you're the center of attraction.
But when you look good, you're going to get some reaction."

For the next 6 hours he cried to his mom.
I said I hope we don't go through this 2 hundred more times.

He's growing up too fast—Hard Head thinks he's a man.
They're all the same, they don't listen. Kids just don't understand.

We were on our vacation, on a beach in Bimini.
I didn't need a tan, so I checked out the bikinis.

And then the phone call came, long distance from home.
I said "Oh-oh what's happened—let me get to the phone."

The law on the line: "Come and get your son."
I said, "What happened officer? Did he grab my gun?"

It was nothing like that, but I thought it was worse.
He had driven my Porsche. Boy, If I get to him first. . .

I'm going to smack his skinny butt, I'll ring his turkey neck.
But his mother held me back so she could go ahead and check. . .

To see if he had a pulse, if his brain was still working.
'Cause to do something like this, he had to be smoking

Some potato peels, tea leaves or some crap.
But whatever it was I knock it out with a slap. . .

Upside his "acorn head." I don't mean to hurt. Want to teach him
A lesson that will eventually help him.

As it turned out, "Knucklehead" picked up a little girl.
He told her she was so fine, and he could "rock her world."

I said "Boy, are you crazy, with AIDS going around?
You don't know where that girl's been. She's from the wrong
side of town."

She put her hand on his knee, he put his foot on the gas.
I couldn't take no more. I was ready to kick the a—z. . .

Cut off the top of his head. . .How could he be so dumb?
And
With the cops on his heels, he thought he could out run the man.

Are you sick, boy? you can never hide,
'Cause if they miss you, I'll get you, and I won't back slide!
(You hear me!)

I know kids are human, and they'll make mistakes.
But when you do stupid stuff, that I can't take!

I try to school the boy—to teach him right from wrong,
But when you pick up little girls, it won't be too long.

You'll have a child of your own, a ball and chain on your neck.
And you'll wish you had listened, gave me some respect.

I love my boy with all my heart until the day I die.
But leave my Porsche alone. . .don't even try to drive it.

He's trying to grow up too fast. Hard Head thinks he's a man.
They're all the same—Kids don't listen, kids just don't understand!!

OVERWEIGHT

Size "6" is nice, but add 6—that's mine.
Size 12? I'm big! But I think I'm fine.

Whatever I eat seems to go to my hips.
And thighs, and arms, chest, face and lips.

Food tastes good! Can't put the fork down.
Just one more Twinkie—oops! One more pound.

I luu-vvv to eat! I'm fat and I'm happy!
Got plenty of skin but it's tight, not flabby!

I can gain weight from just looking at food.
I seem to absorb it when I get in the mood.

And do not let me breathe in the aroma.
If I see it! Watch out! My mouth starts to foam-a.

But Hey! Being fat can have its advantages.
Except when there's an accident I'll need more bandages.

When you're thin you get hit and break in half.
Hit me! Don't worry. I'll absorb it and laugh!

Watch me dance! I love to do the "bump."
I command respect with the push from my rump.

I can't understand how you can be small.
Do you ever eat or gain weight at all?

You know, being fat is not always this funny.
I laugh at myself but when you laugh, it hurts, honey.

Laugh "with" me—not "at" me—and take me as I am.
I can't snap my fingers and be thin like you, ma'am.

So don't watch the "waves" that wash in my sea.
Admire my "motion-in-the-ocean" and like me for "me"!

TRAINER

Uh-oh. . .it's time to go back to school.
I'll see all my friends—make some new ones too.

Janie's got zits but she's the same otherwise.
And check out Joanne . . .she's wearing a new size.

And what are those things sticking out of her chest?
Oh no! Joanne has grown some breasts!

Oh my goodness! She looks like a teenager.
She's got the biggest chest in our class of 4th graders.

What did she do to grow 'em? Eat Corn Flakes?
I *must* know her secret. I'll do whatever it takes.

And I'm not even wearing a training bra.
Look at her! She busting out of hers by far.

Uh-oh! My chest is hurting. . .this could be it!
There's a bump! Now I need a "trainer" that fits!

I've got to have breasts! It's the way to go.
Life's tough in the 4th grade—you just don't know!

ZITS

Oh no! I want to scream! I've got a zit on my face.
Right on the forehead and that's the worst place.

And there's one on the side near the cheek bone.
And another on the chin—it must have just grown.

I've got to go to school—oh no, I can't believe it!
That big ugly thing is right where they all can see it.

Do I dare pop it? Try to make it go away?
But what if it gets bigger? I think I need to pray.

The kids will laugh I know! Call me "crater face."
And I can not hide—I know of no good place.

I know what I'll do. I'll comb my hair low.
No—that won't work. I'll look like Bozo.

How about this idea? I'll wear a bandaid?
And if my friends should ask, I was cut by a blade.

I'll tell them the robber was big! He tried to slice me.
As he took my money he almost "diced me."

No, that doesn't feel right—yeah, that would be lying.
I guess I'll have to bear it even though I'm crying.

I know this is a phase . . .I hope I get over it.
But why me, why now? Why must I get this zit?

PHONE

Mom, Kris is on the phone again
She's in love again
Gonna tie up the line all night

Mom. . .Kris has your makeup on
Her skirt is not that long
And I think it's too tight

Mom. . .Kris is trying to wear high heels
And I think she did steal
Your diamond earrings too!

Mom. . .Kris is using your perfume
I could smell it on the moon
And she told me you knew

Mom. . .Kris swung at me with a brush
And I think I should rush
Right out of your room!

Mom. . .Gee I thought you wanted me to
Tell—I guess not, oh well. . .
I think I'd better split soon!

ITCH

Uh-oh I feel an "itch" and I don't know how to scratch it.
Girls look diff'rent now. . . Is it hair? Perfume? Yeah that's it.

My voice is getting deeper. . . I sang tenor, now it's bass.
I think I need a shave—Look! Two hairs on my face!

Girls used to be just dummies—they really got
on my nerves.
But now I like to be near them—they were flat, now they
have curves.

I used to pull their hair. . .couldn't stand to be
around them.
And now I look in a crowd and I'm happy when I've
found them.

I find myself staring at a girl in my class
Does she think I'm cute? Should I speak or let her pass?

Hmmm— What would I say? "Hello, nice weather we're
having"?
She'll really think I'm a dork, then she'll walk away
laughing.

I've got a strange feeling—My "insides" are starting to
"twitch"
Suddenly girls look good. . .Are they causing this
itch?

NONDANCER

I like M.C. Hammer when he "shakes and bakes."
The Soul Train dancers certainly have what it takes.
The kids at school leave me in a trance.
But my problem is *I just can't dance!*

Three years late, but now I've got the "slide"
But my friends stopped doin' it. . .that's hurt my pride.
They learn the other dances like there's nothing to it.
But when I tried to dance I just blew it.

Do you know what it's like to be in the crowd
With the music pumpin' the jams out loud?
Everybody's throwin' down with the latest moves.
And I'm a "wall flower" 'cause I got no groove.

I have all kinds of problems 'cause I can't dance.
It limits my chances at finding romance.
What do I do when they play a slow jam?
I can't slow dance either. Do you understand?

I'll skip math study for my dance practice.
If Fred Astaire could do it I can hack this.
I'll flunk math but I'll look good on the floor!
Mom'll kill me! Oh well. . .I'll worry no more.

CAR

(kid:)
Catching the bus is a drag—I need a "RIDE!"
Walking to school or to work? I got my PRIDE!
My very own car would be nice! I could GLIDE!
Isn't a car a "benefit" parents PROVIDE?

(Parent:)
So you want a car by 16? You amaze me!
Do you know what a car costs? Are you crazy?
The "note," insurance and gas? And who pays the
Bills? Be thankful for "legs." Don't be lazy!

(kid:)
My friend has his very own car—he's RIDING!
His mom and dad paid his bill. NO JIVING!
He goes where he wants when he wants—I'm not LYING.
It's only fair I get a car—Dad, I'm DYING!

(parent:)
You talk about driving your car and being cool. . .
I can see we've got a lot of work we need to do.
It's a big responsibility—not for a fool.
Maybe you'll get one if you do well in school.

(kid:)
If I get an "A" in Math—will that COUNT?
I could work hard at McDonald's for an AMOUNT. . .
To help pay the down-payment on my ACCOUNT. . .
And in the meantime could I take your CAR OUT?

(parent:)
I always knew this day would come—so you're ready?
Okay. Get behind the wheel—keep your hands steady!
I hope it's the right thing to do 'cause, Freddy—
Your life—and my car—are in your hands—you heard me!

CLOTHES

No ma—please! Don't throw my pants in the trash.
They're not too old and raggedy.
Believe me when I say, "This is the style!"
Losing my jeans would be tragedy!

No ma—please! I can't put on that wool sweater!
It looks like I'm wearing a "bear."
And those bell bottom pants died twenty years ago
They're as out of fashion as long hair!

No ma—please! Not those "Howdy Doody" shoes!
Believe me—I can't wear those things.
If they aren't too tight—they will look so bad
My feet will fight and scream.

No ma—please! Don't make me wear that wide tie.
And that long collar shirt is sad!
Try this "p-c"—it only costs about forty.
And the knit has a fit that is "bad!"

Hey ma—please! Look at these tennis shoes. . .
Only one "C" note you need to pay.
I can wear them now or when we go to church
And get a second pair for play.

Hey ma—isn't shopping really fun?
And this is just a small load.
After we haul in these threads and shoes
We'll start on my winter wardrobe.

ALLOWANCE
(Dad, I need a raise!)

Pop gave me a nickel and he thought that was cool.
I bought a bubble gum and I took it to school.

The teacher said,"Don't chew bubble gum in my class."
So I had to give it up, throw my gum in the trash.

And when I got home I asked Pop for more money.
I wanted some candy—it feels good in my tummy.

He said "I'm sorry, son, that you spent all your cash.
You've got to learn to make your money last.

"That was your allowance—call it your 'weekly pay.'
You've got to spread it out to last more than a day."

And as I grew older I thought I'd get more.
After all, inflation will keep a kid poor!

Pop increased my allowance—he gave me a raise.
I got five dollars on his pay days.

But by then I couldn't buy hardly anything.
Just one cassette blew out everything.

I said "Pop, I need a raise"—five bucks ain't makin' it.
There's movies and tapes and clothes—I can't fake it.

My pop could say "no" in a thousand different ways.
He'd say "no" with a smile, or "no" through a daze.

He'd be smackin' on chicken and say "no" between bites.
He'd say "no" in the morning—at noon—or at night.

So how do I get Pop to give up the cash?
Do extra dishes. . .Or take out the trash?

Can't get a job. . .I'm too young to work.
And every time I ask. . .I get "no" and a smirk.

I know what I'll do! I'll call 9-1-1!
I'll claim "child abuse." No money—no fun!

GRADES

Got a "D" in Spanish and my parents just didn't
understand.
So there goes TV—movies—phone—and parties. I've been
canned!

Mom didn't care that other kids like me failed Spanish
too.
Just wanted to hear the reason why I failed—that course I
blew.

What I want to know is—why do I always have to get an
"A"?
Parents drive me crazy with the pressure I get
day-to-day.

Is that the only measure of success in the world
today?
I guess no matter how you slice it. . .Nothing beats
an "A."

The teacher is mean! Her breath stinks—plus she walks just
like a man.
And she comes from Georgia—speaking Spanish? I can't
understand.

I gave it all I had—I did! I really tried hard to
pass.
But for some reason nothing worked for me—So I failed the
class.

I just could not get past the "U-NO-DOS-TRES-
QUATRO"—
I have enough trouble speaking English—a language I should
know!

And why do I need Spanish when all my friends are talking
Greek?
Could it help me find a job in a city where Spanish they
speak?

In Florida, Cally, and Texas, I guess you need to know that
stuff.
'Cause having a diploma in liberal arts won't be
enough!

I might go to Spain one day and talk with the native
Senoritas.
Sit in the shade and have a couple of nice-cold
margaritas.

Hmmm, suddenly my studying Spanish might not be bad
after all!
I may just get that "A" and then I'll go out and have
a ball!

But is that the only measure of success in the world
today?
I guess no matter how you slice it—trust me—nothin' beats
an "A"!

SQUEALER

Oooooooooh! I saw you and—yeah—I'm tellin'!
When mom finds out at you she'll be yellin'.
She'll smack your butt and it will be swellin'.
You blew it this time—and yeah—I'm tellin'!

Yeah "home girl," you're in trouble now!
I can hear that belt hittin' your butt—pow!
No more TV, or phone calls for a while.
Yeah big sis—you're in big trouble now.

You thought you were slick, but not slick enough.
I saw you and I'm tellin, and babe that's tough!
No need to beg, 'cause you're embarrassed, cream puff.
You're in big trouble now—hey, life is rough!

I'm just doing my job as a little brother.
I'm not a weasel—just doin' what any other
Kid would do when his sister didn't cover
Or correct a mistake that could hurt others.

So you want to call me a squealer?
I don't have to tell. Let's make a deal—uh. . .
Be nice to me sometime so I can feel—uh—
Like I'm okay. I'm your brother not a "pealer."

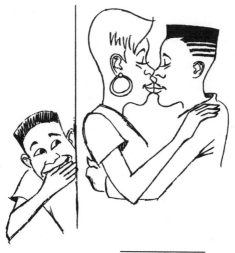

NAME GAME
(It's no fun)

How do you feel when someone calls you a name?
Like "fat head," "big butt," or "ugly"—"plain Jane"?

It hurts like a punch and can leave you lame.
'Cause nobody wins when you play the "name game."

Remember the saying about sticks and stones?
Names hurt other ways without breaking bones.

I know 'bout the pain cause I've been there before.
Guys jump on you—first a little, and then more. . .

They watch your reaction—the silence or tears—
And if you let them they'll be on you for years.

They know where to hit you and names hit so hard.
Finding your weakness and dropping your guard.

They'll test your strength to measure your "core"
And if you let them they'll go on and score.

So how do you win at this stupid game?
Does anyone win when you're hurt with a name?

Try to ignore it! Give'em no satisfaction.
Don't tell them they've scored by your "hurt" reaction.

Should you fight back with some words just as tough?
Be ready to run in case they want to get rough!

You know what they say about turning the other cheek?
You can still be strong. Silence doesn't mean you're weak.

Take it for now—you'll grow out of it yet.
And pay them no mind 'cause that's the safe bet. . .

Don't worry about things that you cannot change.
Don't waste your time playing their silly games.

Just grin and bear it—don't trouble yourself.
Look at your good side for that is your wealth.

Part IV
Cashin' In

LOTTO FEVER

They stood near the counter. . .The small crowd of five. . .
In spirited discussion—this talk was "live."

Tension filled the air as the talkers got hot. . .
I thought, any moment, someone could get shot.

The volume of voices continued to rise. . .
And sweat from the brow dripped in their eyes.

It was clear the argument would soon come to head. . .
If no one backed down, would someone be dead?

One argued logic, the other emotion. . .
She knew she was right, while he had a "notion".

No one backed away from a stated view. . .
They all were right. . .but they were wrong too.

Still it got hotter. . .from the unfolding drama. . .
She called him a name. . .He cursed her momma.

Finally they tired and decided to quit. . .
They all left the store before someone got hit.

And what was all the fussing about?
Why the number "2"—not the "8"—came out.

MONEY

Why is there so much fuss about money?
It's what makes the world go round, honey.
Try to buy something without it, sonny.
Get your feelings hurt—that ain't funny.

Today—tomorrow—and from here on out
You're going to get bombed and that's without a doubt.
"Got to make the money"—going to need it, 'scout'
To survive in this world—that's what it's about.

Study hard then get a good job
That'll pay "big bank" so you won't have to rob
To pay for your clothes—won't look like a slob
Enjoy caviar and eat like a snob.

Be careful, don't get obsessed with it.
Don't try the "drug". . .don't even mess with it
Once you get hooked, you'll need cash for it
And you'll curse yourself for having tested it.

Some people get hooked on money another way.
Got to have the best of everything today—
Put emphasis on the "thing" as if to say
Having "stuff" makes me better than you—hey!

Don't get caught with this wrong interpretation,
Sell your soul for nice transportation,
Abuse your body for temporary sensation,
Or try to impress with a phony revelation

What you'll be then is an empty shell—
You'll have a lot of "toys" but life is hell.
What about real friends? Can't buy them! I tell
You don't burn your bank book with drugs—well. . .

Make money—sure—but make it your "means"
To reach your goal, achieve your dreams.
Times will be tight and sometimes it seems
When you don't have it—you'll want to scream.

Money can't buy true happiness
Or love—the feeling from a sincere caress
Nothing beats the feeling of hard-earned success
Or a gift from God when you are blessed.

GIVING
(How I'm trying to resolve my problem)

Here we go again—"We need more donations.
Please pull out the cash to help our situation."

Light bills are high and the walls need repair.
Poor people are crying, asking if we really care.

And the bishop says he needs more money too. . .
Talking 5 or 10%—who does he think he's talking to?!

Give! Give! Give! It seems like that's all we hear.
Summer, fall, winter, spring—all times of the year.

There's no end to begging from the church and on the job.
Their hands stay in my pockets—it's like pressure from the mob.

What about my needs?—The home, car and kids?
Have you seen my grocery bill? It's like they took the lid. . .

Off the prices. Plus utilities? C'mon—give me a break!
It seems that the "greedy" know, well, how to take.

Luxuries? Try movie rentals at three bucks a shot.
And five more on the lottery—in case I get hot.

I really don't mind giving if it's for a good cause.
So when the church asks I guess I'll have to pause. . .

And think about the reason—are they being greedy?
Or are matters that serious—like more numbers of "needy"?

So what does the Bible say about making a contribution?
Is the amount you give connected with absolution?

One verse says not to "store up your treasures. . .
Where rust and moths destroy" worldly pleasures.

God loves a cheerful giver—or so I am told.
What I give to his people I'll get back ten-fold?

No matter how valuable our possessions may be. . .
We'll have to give them up to enter heaven, you see.

So giving more now didn't hurt my financial health.
I had to firm up my belief of the need to share my wealth.

And you don't have to be rich to give something that counts.
It's the "quality" of the gift—not so much the amount.

Let's say you only had two bucks to your name
And you gave God one—He'd give you more acclaim. . .

Than a millionaire who only drops in a "C-note". . .
Giving of your "substance" will always get God's vote.

Yes it would be nice to throw in lots of cash
But offerings can vary from money to even "trash."

Say you spent twelve bucks on junk food last week.
And dropped coins in the offering with your tongue in cheek.

For the fourth straight weekend you had pizza-to-go
But when collection time came the basket passed your row.

And when you light up a smoke just outside the door,
Blowing 2 bucks in the air just a few feet from the poor. . .

Talking about priorities—take a look at the need. . .
You've seen ads on TV on who five dollars can feed.

There are many ways to give—one especially you will find
More valuable than money—it's the gift of your time!

Visit the sick, feed the poor or join in song.
When giving time to the church you'll never go wrong.

Giving is a requirement of your Christian faith. . .
Give your gift much thought; don't make it in haste.

When you give, feel good! There should be no pain.
Give your wealth and time and many blessings you'll gain.

And when you give alms don't do it for show. . .
Keep your deeds secret—only God needs to know.

Part V
Special People

FAMILY
(The need for "bonding" from a child's eye)

Why does my mother always walk in front of me?
It's like she is ashamed of what people will see.
"Oh—she is so young to have a child in school. . ."
I guess having children sometimes is not so cool.

I wish that she would stop and take me by the hand.
And walk with me like she was proud with me to stand.
Why does my daddy not take the time to play?
I know he works so hard and may be tired today.

It would mean so much if he taught me how to catch.
Or explained to me these feelings like this itch I need to scratch.
I often wish that mom would read me a book. . .
You know, one of those crazy ones like *Snow White* or *Captain Hook*.

I know it must sound corny since I'm growing up so fast,
But every now and then I like the simple things that last.
And what about my dad who only shows up when
I get a bad report card or I'm fighting with a friend?

When I look at Jimmy, who's always on restriction
I get a little jealous because he gets attention.
At least his parents seem to care to keep him out of trouble,
But mine are always busy working one shift, then a double.

The "picture-perfect" family that's often on TV
Is a lot different from what's happening with me.
With mom and dad both working to try to make ends meet,
Sometimes I don't see either one until I go to sleep.

I like to sometimes dream of all of us at play. . .
Or sitting in a church—holding hands as we pray.
And when we have those special—Parent/Teacher meetings. . .
The other-kids'-mom-and-pop-show-up-and-get-to-see-things. . .

That go on at school which—is a part of my life. . .
A part of me that I want to share with them that's nice.
Maybe-one-day-mom-and-pop-will-see-what's-important-to-me. . .
And instead of being divided like "he," "she," "they," it's "WE."

ADOPTION: A CHILD'S WISH

As you look at my picture in the adoption book. . .
What do you see? What do you think of my look?

If I'm smiling it's 'cause I'm thinking of home.
A place I can go that I'll call my own.

If I'm frowning maybe it's too hard to smile.
I haven't had a reason to laugh in a while.

You may be wondering—why am I here?
Did my parents do something to cause a tear?

Was I neglected—a victim of abuse?
By a mom or pop who had a short fuse?

Or am I sick with some kind of affliction?
Did my birth mother have a drug addiction?

As you look, why keep asking what's wrong?
It's not my fault—I haven't lived that long.

But if given a chance I think that I might
Grow up to be very strong and bright.

Whatever my situation, it's no fault of my own.
I had no choice on where I called home.

Shuttled from one foster family to another
Sometimes I'm separated from my sister and brother.

Everyday I wonder—what is it like?
To have my own home—parents and a bike.

How does it feel to have a "real" family?
Someone to love and spend time with me?

I'd love to have a daddy—whatever that means.
A real one just like on the TV screens.

And a mother that will cry when I get sick.
Or slap my hand when my nose I pick.

Sometimes I'm scared about my adoption.
Will you like me and love me and forget the option. . .

To send me back if I don't act right?
Just give me a chance I'll try with my might.

If you're worried about cost—I'm an investment.
Your dividend will be all of my love as a present.

So, look twice at my picture in the adoption book. . .
Think about what really is behind my "look."

I just want a chance to have what you've got. . .
A family of my own that will love me a lot.

BLACK, WHITE, OTHER?

(Thoughts about my brother's marriage to a German woman—
shared with an organization of interracial couples and families)

On the application form there was a box to check
Question: "Black, White, Other?". . .Asking "race" I suspect.

But isn't that illegal in this free and just nation?
Or does it depend on how they use the information?

"Black, White, Other?". . .Your kids will know that question well
But how they respond is another story to tell.

What do you teach them? What reasoning do you use?
Is it painful to decide? Or do you simply refuse?

It's a shame we have to ask. . .But it's the times we're livin'
"Inquiring minds want to know." So what answers are you givin'?

"Black, White, Other?". . .Why do they need to know?
In a society of labels it's their right to intrude, so. . .

You are polite. . .Or you ignore the query
But it sticks in your mind and may cause you to worry

Do you have to answer? What purpose is served?
To demand a response—or simply impose one—what nerve!

You knew this would happen but, when blinded by love,
You said, "We'll cross that bridge in time with help from above."

Your union shows us all what's right in this day
Not blinded by color, letting love lead the way.

Still those nagging questions from strangers and "friends"
And family above all—some don't want to comprehend.

You think long and hard and ask for God's help
You pray for sensitivity, understanding, and what else?

The strength to endure. . .Ignorance. . .Ridicule
To believe you are right. . .That your love is a jewel.

Many will never understand you, but some of us will
Those who don't care about skin color—or labels and frill.

Now—to deal with responsibility of history and future
What will you teach the child—what lessons will nurture?

About blacks, about whites. . .The child will need your strength
To feel comfortable with himself—and live life as it's meant. . .

Well, the time is now—for the children of you
You have chosen an answer . . .You've thought this through

"Black, White, Other?". . .What box will you check?
'Til you get a better choice, mark all three! What the heck!

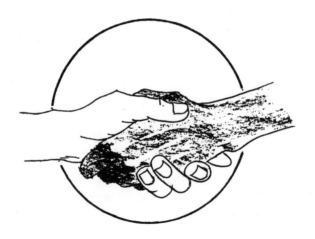

SPECIAL D

Let me tell you the story of a kid named Special D
He thought he was "regular," not a star—'xcuse me.

Now, all Special D wanted was just to fit in—
You know, be one of the boys, run the girlies and win. . .

At basketball and some of the games people play
He just wanted to be accepted by the kids around the way.

Couldn't sing like "Bel Biv" or dance like "Heavy D"
But he had his faded hair cut—and hundred-dollar "Nikey"

Now—Special D was no dummy—he was smart as a whip
Could run through his homework, read and understand the
trip. . .

Through the world of ideas—people, places and things.
Had ideas of his own, but no one looked at his ring. . .

Of thought. But Special D liked to play, and be cool—
So much so, he missed out on assignments in school.

He failed four classes in his first semester alone!
Dropped three more the next, and was not afraid to go home.

Why? He had "accelerated" courses, so mom cut him some
slack.
And he played it to the hilt—saying he need room to "relax."

Ninth grade was wasted, and Special D didn't care.
Well, he said he didn't, but deep down in here. . .

He knew he could ace science, history and math
But the fellas called him nerdy, if he did well, and passed.

About tomorrow? His future, Special D had no clue
Like most kids, he lived for today—like some of you.

And then one day, as he was lunchin' in the caf'
He heard a strange sound that kind of made him laugh.

Some kids were on the mike, trying to rock the "P-A"
But they didn't have a clue on what to do or say.

Now Special D could read, and he had an okay voice
And he could join that club—if it was his choice.

Nuthin' to it but to do it. . .So he did. Special D
Signed up for the club, rocked and rolled with a new buddy (the mike).

He had to read announcements—play music and speak
To all the kids in the school, while they were lunchin' at peak.

Special D liked that job, and he did it very well
So well in fact, a teacher called him in to tell. . .

Him to keep up the good work, and think of a career,
As a disc jockey, on radio or even TV. "I hear. . .

People reading news, selling cars and making big money.
You could do the same," he said, "if you're serious, not funny"

Special D liked that thought, of having "big bank,"
From doing easy work on the mike—so he thanked. . .

The teacher for the advice. And he went on and did his 'do.'
He rocked the "P-A" as best he could, too.

He'd listen to the radio and say—hey, I can do that.
And he'd practice the techniques of reading and "rap."

He enjoyed it so much—it affected all other work
Suddenly he wanted to do well. . .D's and F's were for jerks.

Felt good to get an A—should have done it all along.
Almost made the honor roll, believe it? And nothing was wrong.

Special D was finally doing what he knew was right
Doing his best—showing his talents—he really was bright.

So what made him "special"? What really earned him the name?
He's Special D the D-J, and newsman—no fame!

No, not yet, but then—that's not what's it's all about, you see.
I just want to be productive, creative, and happy.

KRIS
(Stepdaughter)

You were five when we married
I wasn't there when mom carried
You in her bosom—
A long time it's been.

You knew your "real" father
I thought it would bother
You. . .When the time came
And I moved in.
We needed time to get used to
Each other and you too
Were nervous like me
But still. . .

I'll never forget when
One day we were talkin'
You called me "daddy"
What a thrill!

Your smile is so bright
We could use it to light
Up the house
On a gloomy day.

But on the other hand
Sometimes we can't stand
Your pouting when
You don't get your way.

I just want to reach you. . .
And try to teach you
Some things about life
And what it takes. . .

You're at the age now
When you can see how
Life comes together
You make your breaks.

You've got so much going. . .
Brains, looks, and enjoying
the other kids' attention
you're really cool. . .

But life's about more
Than just keeping score
On who's got the smoothest
Guy in high school.

You like to get phone calls
And spend time in the malls
Have plenty fun now. . .
And that's okay. . .

Be ready to draw the line
'Cause in a short time
It'll soon be your turn
To pay your way.

I know the pressure is tough
And the kids can be rough
On those who don't try
Sex and Blow. . .

But back to my preachin'
Until I am reachin'—
You. Kris—these are things
you need to know.

You have so much to live for
With your brains you can score
Very well on
Any kind test. . .

All you have to do
Is make up your mind to
Give it your all
And be the best.

Use all of your mind.
And soon you will find
Rewards come your way
When you excel. . .

When you have talent
You'd better use it
Take pride in
Doing anything well

We will keep trying
'Til we bore you to crying
To help you want to
Have the "best."

It doesn't come easy
Don't settle for sleazy
If it's worth it—you've
Gotta pass a test.

You have to "want to". . .
We know we can't force you
To excel at
Everything you try.

But if you do so
The rewards you will know
And you'll thank us 'til
The day you die. . .

Hey. . .There's one more thing
I'll "say" it. . .I can't sing
Never forget this
It comes from above

As long as I live
I'll do my best to give
You—unconditionally—
All of my love. . .

KEITH

(at the funeral of Keith Raynard Scott, Jr., 3/27/89)

Note: "Little Keith," as he was known to family and friends, needed a new liver. So for several months, WRAP radio pushed the "Keith Campaign" to raise money and public awareness. Keith died before the operation could be performed. I read this poem at his funeral.

The sun is shining for a reason. . .
It's not easy to understand. . .
Today we say goodbye to Keith. . .
Farewell to the little man.

His time with us was oh so short. . .
He would have been two on Sunday. . .
But if God's will is to be done,
We'll meet again one day.

Like many of you—I have
children. . .My youngest is a boy. . .
And—to watch him grow up and learn. . .
Is such a heartfelt joy.

Anyone who's ever experienced
The genuine love of a child. . .
Knows the joy in watching him
Wake up or even smile.

So it was easy to say "yes" when
Keith's mom Jackie called to say. . .
"Little Keith needed a new liver. . ."
And she knew she could not pay.

The quarter-million-dollar price—
A transplant was going to cost.
But without the operation
Keith's battle was lost.

And throughout the next ten months,
Our station put out the call. . .
"Little Keith needs your help—
Send money—but pray above all. . ."

Because now it doesn't matter
How sick a person may be. . .
The question is who has the money
To pay the high medical fee.

But Jackie was like any mother—
Determined to find a way. . .
To do everything in her power
So that Keith might see the day. . .

When people care, and people share
And reach out to their fellow man. . .
Not worrying about your status or worth—
Offering that helping hand.

Jackie came to our studios—
Sometimes six in the morning—
To tell her story to whomever thought
A child in need was not boring.

And slowly but surely, people gave—
A nickel—a dime—and more. . .
They knew that Keith could have been
Their child—so the love began to pour.

As the dollars started to add up—
It seemed God gave Keith more time. . .
I'd call Jackie to see how he's doing. . .
She'd say, "Oh, he's doing just fine."

He tried to play and act just like
The other kids would do. . .
But God still had a plan for Keith. . .
"No more pain or suffering for you."

And when God did call him home that day—
Believe me—it cut like a knife. . .
Until we finally understood—
Keith now has eternal life.

Where he can run and play and cut up—
Just like the other kids do. . .
Little Keith's in heaven now. . .
Where we wish we all were too.

So—as we wipe away the tears—
That continue to fall. . .
Let us be glad Keith suffers no more. . .
Lets rejoice one and all!

Let's cherish the moments we did have. . .
Although it seems they were few.
Let's learn from the lessons he taught us—
To share, care and love—too.

Let's treasure the memory of his smile—
And let it work for us. . .
Let's open out hearts to the next person
Who needs our love and trust.

The sun is shining for a reason. . .
Though it's not easy to understand.
We should smile at the thought that, maybe
We'll see you soon little man.

Part VI
The "Deal"

WHY (Black History?)

If you find yourself asking,
Why do we have to
Study "Black History" stuff?

We've got enough books about
Our "founding fathers"
The Big Names—aren't they enough?

Well, put yourself in my place
Flip through the pages
Tell me what you really see.

There's Washington, Jefferson
Edison and Bell.
But no one who looks like me!

Ev'ry day that I study—
It grates on my nerves
My folks did nothing worthwhile?

Didn't black people "invent"
And "conquer" and "teach"
And create products with style?

The case for black hist'ry
Is simply a fight—
A struggle for some respect.

'Cause when kids see Black faces
Who have done great things.
The lessons they'll never forget.

ABC'S (of Black History)

In 1770
On a Boston Street
CRISPUS ATTUCKS was the first to die.
At the start of the
Revolutionary War
His effort was a valiant try.

And with their freedom
The new Americans
Needed a capital city.
BENJAMIN BANNECKER—
A surveyor and clock maker—
Helped plan Washington, D.C.

GEORGE WASHINGTON CARVER
Studied the peanut
And his work surprised us so.
This scientist developed
Hundreds of products
From the nut and sweet potato.

And when we needed
A way to preserve
Blood for a lifesaving transfer,
DR. CHARLES DREW
Developed blood banks
That stored plasma—as the answer.

DUKE ELLINGTON was
A conductor, composer
And pianist with a lot of style. . .
His big band jazz
And orchestra sounds
Made millions of music fans smile.

Say: "R-E-S-
P-E-C-T". . .
It was ARETHA FRANKLIN'S hit song. . .
Since the '60s she's been

Called the Queen of Soul;
Her voice is still very strong.

BERRY GORDY started
A record company
In Detroit—he called it Motown. . .
It showcased the
Temptations and Supremes
And more acts with a brand new sound.

ALEX HALEY told the world
His story called *Roots*. . .
It was a monumental book.
And for the first time
It gave many people
A very special inside look. . .

At the system of slavery
And how it affected
A family and a growing nation. . .
It was a very painful
History lesson
Told for today's generation.

REX INGRAM was
A dynamic actor. . .
Despite discrimination against the guy.
This man had good roles
In the movies—*King Kong*
Huck Finn and *Cabin in the Sky*.

In 1935
A Mr. FREDERICK JONES
Developed a new kind of refrigeration.
For trucks and trains
Carrying produce.
It helped farmers across the nation.

"K" should lead you
To think of a man
From Atlanta—we know him as KING.
MARTIN LUTHER
Got a nation to believe
Civil rights was a good thing.

LOUIS LATIMER was
A draftsman by trade
And his electric inventions were exciting.
He helped develop
An incandescent lamp
That gave cities all over new lighting.

Two "M's" to show—
JAN EARNEST MATZELIGER
Was the first to build a machine. . .
That could sew leather
To the sole of a shoe
It was a cobbler's dream.

And did you know
That GARRETT A. MORGAN
Developed the first traffic light?
He also built
The first gas mask
And, to firemen, it was a welcomed sight.

NAT TURNER was a
Handyman—and minister.
His many talents were surprising.
But Nat and others
Were not happy as servants
And they led the first slave uprising.

At the 1936
Olympic games
When Hitler showcased his "master race". . .
JESSIE OWENS won
Three gold medals
Leaving Hitler red in the face.

And you may have heard
The saying that goes—
"Grab a bull by the horns"?
Well, BILL PICKETT
Did just that—
One of the best cowboys ever born.

BENJAMIN QUARLES wrote
Books on black history

He undertook tedious research.
At Morgan State U.
He taught all about
Blacks in science, business and Church.

In 1839,
JOSEPH CINQUE,
The son of a chief, was caught. . .
He led a slave mutiny—
And won their freedom
In a Supreme Court battle he fought.

Outfielder FRANK ROBINSON
Was the only player
To win the "M-V-P". . .
In baseball's American
And National leagues
He was that good—believe me!

In the Civil War,
ROBERT SMALLS and other slaves
Stole a confederate ship. . .
He navigated the hundred-
And-forty-foot boat
To freedom—giving the rebs the slip.

HENRY TANNER had
A special gift—for him
Painting it seemed to come naturally.
His "Resurrection of Lazarus"
Does still hang
In a great French art gallery.

In the 1960s—
For a time
LESLIE UGGAMS was the only black. . .
To be on TV
In a regular role. . .
Singing and dancing with talent she didn't lack.

There's a special place
In music history
For a singer that's simply divine.
SARAH VAUGHN made hits

With her rich deep voice
With jazz or the classics of the time.

Three "W's" now,
The first is WASHINGTON.
We like to call him BOOKER T.
This educator and leader
Started a college
In Alabama, it's called Tuskeegee.

GRANVILLE T. WOODS
Was called the "black Edison"
For his many electrical inventions.
His own factory produced
Telephones, and transmitters
And too many other devices to mention.

MAGGIE WALKER of Richmond
Had a talent for numbers
If you want to be frank.
Ms. Walker was
The first woman in the U.S.
To be president of a chartered bank.

"X" is for MALCOLM LITTLE—
We call him MALCOLM X.
Leader who dared to say—
African Americans
Are special people
Who should and could find their own way.

In the Spanish American War,
CHARLES YOUNG
Led some courageous fighters. . .
The army major
And his regiment
Saved Teddy Roosevelt's Rough Riders.

Last but not least
Is SHAKA ZULU. . .
A great South African man. . .
In the early 1800s
He made the Zulu nation
the most powerful in the land.

So there you have it,
Just a few of the names—
Of some blacks who were a mystery.
There are many more—
Check your library or store
For the A-B-C's of black history.

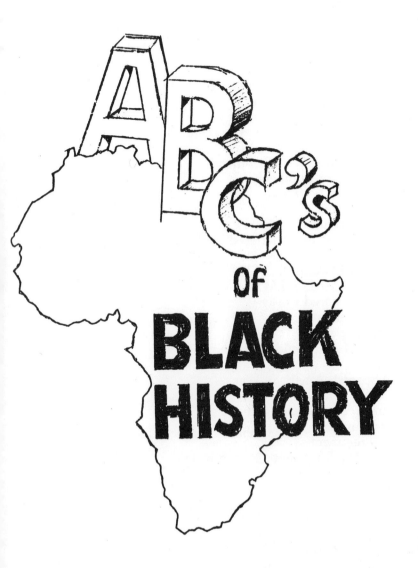

KING

Why do we honor Martin as if he were a *King*?
We treat him like Royalty, but he was no such thing.

We've reserved the third Monday of the first month of
the year
As a day to remember Martin and what he fought for
without fear.

No "blue blood" in this *King*'s veins like rich and famous
types.
His family tree *was* special but without all
the hype.

Most "kings" can trace their roots back to medieval time.
But slavery cut Martin's family tree off at the vine.

That did not stop Daddy *King* and Alberta from doing
their best
To prepare M.L., A.D. and Christine for life's
ultimate test.

Martin's parents stressed education and in school he did real
well.
He developed a love for learning and was determined to
excel.

But separate schools for blacks and whites were the law of
the land.
No integration unless Negro services were
in demand.

The more Martin learned about life, the more he questioned
Why?
Why coloreds, Negroes, Blacks and African children had to
cry.

And while some *Kings* rule a nation—their word is
absolute. . .
Martin preached in any church trying to reach
a few.

All because he believed that we could live together. . .
All kinds of people: Black, White, Protestant, Jew, whatever.

But, is that, alone, enough to earn Martin a crown?
Ranked up there with James and Henry—*Kings* of such renown?

There was faith in his home—Daddy King was a preacher
And his mother shared her talents, serving as a music teacher.

But, *kings*, as we know them, live in luxury and
splendor.
Martin and Coretta rented a house. And in a way he was a
vendor.

His "wares" were in the Bible—he offered God's word to
people
Working out of a Montgomery church that had a magnificent
steeple.

He was pretty comfortable, with a rich black congregation,
A Ph.d. and new baby—he had a good situation.

But when Ms. Rosa Parks, with her tired feet
and all,
Was told she had to give up her seat on the bus "'cause
y'all—

Nigras have to stand!" and that's the way it was
Rosa went to jail—and Martin had a "cause". . .

A reason to speak up to try and right the wrong—
This young man fresh from Morehouse and Boston U. was strong.

Filled with determination to try and make a change
He did have doubts about reaching for something out of range.

And then he "met" Mahatma Ghandi who also fought
Oppression from the British in India—and Ghandi taught—

Martin how to win over the powerful, evil force.
Without using guns—But it was no easy course.

Ghandi preached nonviolence, saying Love will change their hearts.
That changed Martin forever and he continued to do his part.

He walked the streets of Memphis with the jobless and
oppressed.
Have you ever seen a *king* do that? They ignore any kind of
mess.

Martin fought off rocks and bottles, biting dogs, and hoses. . .
And standing up to racial hatred was no bed of roses.

He frequently landed in jail, but Martin used a pen
While in Birmingham's lockup—it was that time when. . .

He wrote a letter to his fellow brothers of the cloth. . .
Those, fearing for their lives, who urged him to back off.

That "Letter from Birmingham Jail" called them to do what
they must—
"Any law that degrades human personality
is unjust."

To prove a point Martin organized The March on D.C.. . .
A quarter million heard his cry that all men need to be free.

It was a Dream he dared to have for black 'n' white girls and
boys. . .
To see them walking hand in hand, experiencing youthful
joys.

And—just like a *king*—Martin eventually got his prize. . .
Equal Rights for his people—a new law on his side.

In '64 the president signed a major Civil Rights Bill.
And Martin earned the Nobel Prize for Peace—it was a thrill.

But all the prizes and new laws did not change attitudes.
Tears still fell from wrongs and peaceful protest became bad
news.

Younger blacks filled with pride grew tired of taking abuse.
Martin cried when their riots and shootings headlined the news.

And on that fateful evening—April 4, in
'68—
In Memphis around six pm as he was leaving for a speaking
date. . .

A shotgun blast knocked him down while at Lorraine Motel.
This man of peace was killed and now his story we tell.

We proudly honor Martin because he was a *king*.
We rightfully take a day off to acknowledge that he was willing. . .

To do the ultimate—to die for what he believed. . .
To give his most valuable possession—his life. So, he receives. . .

A crown of jewels more valuable than anything on this earth.
His true reward is in heaven—no price measures its worth.

The fight he led for freedom, justice and a fair shake. . .
For people he's never met, the children with futures at
stake. . .

Is finally coming true. Just watch little kids at play.
They know no color barriers. . .except what their parents say.

The numbers are improving—just take a look
around you.
More and more, you're getting the chance to show what you
can do.

Slowly but surely we're seeing more of us offering that
helping hand
Thanks to a *King*, we're on our way to reaching the
Promised Land.

X-MAN

You wear the hat up on your head because you think it's
cool.
But when I ask you what it means, why do you say "Who?"

Brother, Sister—Time to sit down and go back to school.
'Cause—to *not* know Malcolm X makes you look like a fool.

He was an agitator—instigator—an angry man.
But he also tried to help his People understand.

He said be proud that your ancestral roots are African
And use your pride in yourself to be the best you can.

Go back now for a quick review of recent history.
About this man who, to many people, is still a mystery.

Had a Bad Attitude 'cause his own people did not see
How they were taught to hate themselves and fight unity.

Before the "X" this Malcolm was Mr. Earl Little's man.
Born in 1925 the son of a Preacher Man.

In Omaha, Nebraska, the hate was a lot more than
His family could take so they moved away to Michigan.

In '31 a streetcar ran over his father and killed him one day!
But that didn't explain why the side of his face was knocked away.

An Accident? Mom didn't think so. Thought it was
K-K-K.
You see, back then white people didn't like what Earl Little
had to say.

He preached Independence, saying you've gotta work to "be
your own boss."
Like Marcus Garvey before him, Earl Little wanted to
sail across. . .

The Atlantic Ocean back to Africa the homeland lost.
To start life fresh, find his roots it'd be worth the cost.

Earl Little's death left mom and kids with very little money.
Nine brothers and sisters had to struggle and it wasn't funny.

Mom got harassed by the Welfare folks who called her
"honey."
It seemed like it rained bad news all the time—Life wasn't
sunny.

Mother Louise couldn't take the pressure. So, she was
committed.
They sent her sons and daughters to foster homes—some
benefitted.

But Malcolm was angry at the break up but he tried to deal with it.
The frustration would last a lifetime, 'cause he refused to forget it.

Back in high school Malcolm Little wanted to be
an attorney.
But an English teacher said, "Work with your hands to get
your money."

Frustrated again he moved to Boston to start a new
journey.
He shined some shoes then turned to drugs, pimping and
burglary!

Malcolm went to prison from 1946 to 1952.
A downer, yes, but he used that time to go back to school.

He learned about Elijah Muhammed. He thought that his
ideas were cool.
Muhammed taught through Islam that Blacks were a superior
race, too.

He started thinking more about how his family was
mistreated by whites.
Then he really got mad about how he'd been
denied his rights.

He learned about slavery how blacks were taught that they
were not bright.
And the lack of any Black History hurt him like
a painful bite.

He joined the Nation of Islam while in Detroit City.
He changed his name to Malcolm X so he could omit the. . .

"Little"—slave—name. "X" stood for his African tribe—the one he
Would never know. So began his service in the Muslim ministry.

Malcolm toured the nation educating and trying to motivate
Other blacks who didn't like being victims of violence and hate.

He organized Temples in Boston and Philly—Elijah thought this was great.
His message was simple—Self-determination can
no longer wait.

The "X-man" clashed with another black leader by the name of King.
Fight racism with love? Not for Malcolm X! Self-defense was his Thing.

President Kennedy was killed. Malcolm tried to speak but his words did sting.
He was suspended by Elijah Muhammad—more tension that did bring.

Malcolm later believed that Muhammad had lied—was a hypocrite.
He felt his brothers were setting him up to one day
take a hit.

Frustrated again he went to Mecca on a very special trip.
To learn about true Moslem beliefs, the pilgrimage was it.

In Mecca, Malcolm met many Moslems with all shades of color.
They treated each other equally, like real sisters and brothers.

The pilgrimage taught him something special—we can live with each other.
With respect for our differences and offer to help
one another.

The "X-MAN" tried to form his own groups—Elijah didn't like that jazz.

And Malcolm changed his name again—EL HAJJ MALIK EL SHABAZZ.

EL HAJJ did mean that he made the trip to the
holy sands.
MALIK was like Malcolm—SHABAZZ a new family name
for this man.

X-MAN no more—he had new ideas when he returned
to the states.
As soon as he landed reporters questioned: "The white man—
Do you still hate?"

The blanket indictment he made no more—he refused to take
the bait.
Black Muslims here didn't like New Malcolm. Their anger
sealed his fate.

His new message was "DEMAND, NOT BEG!" for rights
from the U.N.
His home was bombed—wife and kids not harmed—and
death threats often came in.

He knew he was being followed by some alleged Black
Muslims
Still he pressed on and prepared to speak at the Audubon in
Harlem.

His pregnant wife watched and his four kids too as three
men stood up with guns.
They aimed their weapons and opened fire, bullets flying
from each one.

Malcolm died right there. The men were arrested but their
deed was done.
They silenced his voice but his message lived on with the
movement he had begun.

Thanks to Malcolm X African Americans were motivated to
speak out.
About the years of hate and painful oppression that left them
with so much doubt.

He was the voice at the right time to help
bring change about.
An angry man—true—but one with a purpose and nerve
enough to speak out.

He was an agitator—instigator—an angry man.
But he also tried to help his People understand.

He said—be proud that your ancestral roots are African
And use your pride in yourself to be the best you can.

FREEDOM

You may be wond'ring what the pomp and circumstance is
all about. . .
Old papers signed by dead presidents with big words we
need to shout?

If you never had to do without it you really don't know
what it is.
You may not realize how good it can be until you lose this
FREEDOM biz. . .

FREEDOM! 200 years ago a hungry group of people was
ready to fight—
And die for the chance to live and work and pray 'cause it
was their right!

But years after that this colony forgot what *FREEDOM* really
did mean.
They held thousands of men and women and kids 'cause
slaves didn't have their own dreams.

In 1863 slaves got their wish when Lincoln decreed
EMANCIPATION!
Their birthright was finally the law—*FREEDOM* with that
proclamation.

Since that time we've seen communism hit its stride
then crash.
The people demanded a brand new order—that bankrupt
system didn't last.

Today they say we won't appreciate our good thing 'til we
lose it.
This thing the Chinese and Black South Africans are dying
for the right to choose it.

In South Africa today, millions can't vote—a man has few
choices in his life.
Can't go to good schools or even own a gun—two reasons
why there's strife.

China's is the largest country in the world—but they can't do as we've done
In Tiananmen Square in 1989 some died as they marched for *FREEDOM!*

25 years ago we fought our own battles singing *"We Shall Overcome!"*
We kept on singing and marching, protesting 'til Civil Rights were won!

We have to be vigilant protecting the rights because you never know. . .
When the power hungry, the greedy and insane can somehow grab control.

So when you look at these old papers at the venerable shrine
Think of the price that our people paid for the rights that are yours and mine.

FREEDOM! FREEDOM! FREEDOM! FREEDOM!!! Go 'head and say it one more time.
FREEDOM! Count your lucky stars and say a prayer of thanks 'cause it didn't cost you a dime.

So when you laugh and play or even set your sights on achieving impossible dreams. . .
Now and then, stop. . .and take a minute to think about what it all means.

FREEDOM!

Part VII

Black History Play for a Class or Group

A successful program focusing on Black History can be presented, with group participation, incorporating several of the raps into a play script. The following play is built around these raps:

1. "ABC's of Black History"
(13 kids present 2 letters each, alternating.)

2. "Malcolm X"
(Presented by individual rapper)

3. "King"
(Presented by individual rapper)

4. "Special"
(Presented by individual rapper)

Black History
Script

KIDS MARCH IN, CHANTING.

CHORUS:

It's His-to-ry, shouldn't be a mys-te-ry.
The stories of black people are really special to me.

Lost, stolen, destroyed, or not recorded in my book?
Black achievements are many, but *why* do I have to look—
so hard. . .

History! Shouldn't be a mys-te-ry.
The stories of black people are really special to me.

Lost, stolen, destroyed, or not recorded in my book?
Black achievements are many, but *why* do I have to look—
so hard. . .

(REPEAT UNTIL REACHING STAGE)

INTRO BY LEAD RAPPER #1 (change beat):

Why is it that Black History has to be such a mystery?
The stories of my people lost, stolen, ignored. . .
It's as if history writers got to my folks and got bored.

G.W. is cool. . .of this nation he's the father.
TOMMY J. is okay. Big-time writer, president, scholar. . .

But when I take a look at them—you wanna know what I see?
People who did great things, but they sure don't look like me!

So what does that mean? That my people did nothing great?
I know that's not true—so my books are out of date!

CHORUS (change beat):

Time to get updated, 'cuz.
Time to get updated, 'cuz.
Re-write the history books
And tell the world how it really was.
We're not asking you to turn
"Vanilla suburbs" into "chocolate city"
Just let the record show—
Multi-cultural diversity.

LEAD RAPPER #2

At the beginning we shall start. . .
Like a first grader: "a- b- c. . ."
Listen to some of the names
Of history-makers that look like me:

(13 KIDS LINE UP, STILL ROCKING TO THE BEAT. EACH ONE STEPS FORWARD IN TURN TO RECITE A STANZA OF "THE ABC'S OF BLACK HISTORY.")

LEAD RAPPER #2:

So there you have it—from A To Z
A few of the great people who look like me. . .

But what each one did just wasn't a black thing. . .
The "bell" of their success—throughout the land it does ring.

LEAD RAPPER #1:

Now let's take a moment to single out a few names. . .
Of people who did great things but just not for the fame.

Talkin' 'bout Malcolm and Martin—call them the "M & M Boys."
Their lives touched us all with their trials and their joys.

INDIVIDUAL RAPPER #1 RECITES "X-MAN."

INDIVIDUAL RAPPER #2 RECITES "KING."

INDIVIDUAL RAPPER:

Now I challenge *you* to be history maker.
Do you qualify? Are you special, or a "faker"?
Take this pop quiz on life. Ask yourself
These questions. And the answers will prove your wealth.

INDIVIDUAL RAPPER PRESENTS "SPECIAL."

ALL KIDS CHANT, MARCHING:

It's His-to-ry, shouldn't be a mys-te-ry.
The stories of black people are really special to me.

Lost, stolen, destroyed, or not recorded in my book?
Black achievements are many, but *why* do I have to
look—
so hard. . .

History! Shouldn't be a mys-te-ry.
The stories of black people are really special to me.

Lost, stolen, destroyed, or not recorded in my book?
Black achievements are many, but *why* do I have to
look—
so hard. . .

Please understand why I really need to know.
When I see what they did I just want to say
WHO-O-O-O-O-O-O-OA!

If Johnson, Jackson, and Jordan, Wilder and King
can achieve. . .
I know I can do my thing—I just have to believe. . .
IN ME!

Please understand why I really need to know.
When I see what they did I just want to say
WHO-O-O-O-O-O-O-OA!

If Johnson, Jackson, and Jordan, Wilder and King
can achieve. . .
I know I can do my thing—I just have to believe. . .
IN ME!

—END—